RENT TO OWN
Essential Guide for Homebuyers

Rachel Oliver
&
Neil Oliver

Copyright © 2014 by Neil Oliver and Rachel Oliver

All rights reserved. No part of this publication may be reproduced, distributed or transmitted in any form or by any means, including photocopying, recording, or other electronic or mechanical methods, without the prior written permission of the authors, except in the case of brief quotations embodied in critical reviews and certain other noncommercial uses permitted by copyright law.

Rent to own essential guide for homebuyers / Rachel Oliver Neil Oliver.

ISBN 978-0-9921592-0-7

For permission requests, send an email to: **info@renting2own.ca**
For more information about rent to own, visit our website: **www.renting2own.ca**
Follow us on Twitter: **https://twitter.com/cloverprops**
Claim your free gifts that come with purchase of this book email: **info@renting2own.ca**

This book is designed to provide educational and authoritative information on the subject of renting to own residential real estate. The situations described throughout the book are based on true stories or circumstances. In the interest of protecting the privacy of the individuals whose stories we share, pseudonyms where used. By publishing this book the authors do not offer legal, accounting or financing advice or services. Concerns or questions related to rent to own that are specific to your individual situation should be addressed by appropriate professionals in your local area. The authors of this book are not to be held liable for loss or risk that may be incurred as a direct or indirect consequence of utilizing the information in this book.

For Abbey and Riley.
You inspire us to reach higher and to make a difference.

HOW TO RECOGNIZE A RENT TO OWN SCAM AND PROTECT YOUR MONEY — 47

The Warning Signs — 50
How To Protect Yourself — 51

WILL *YOU* QUALIFY FOR RENT TO OWN? — 53

Qualification Criteria — 54

THE KEY TO SAVING MONEY WHEN YOU RENT TO OWN — 59

What's Included in a Home Inspection? — 61

THE ABC'S OF RENT TO OWN AGREEMENTS — 63

How the Agreements Protect You — 64
The Most Important Agreement — 66
Purchase Ahead of Schedule — 67
What You Need to Know About the Lease Agreement — 67
Get Legal Advice Before Paying Rent to Own Dues — 68

THE 18 RULES OF SUCCESS — 71

MORTGAGE BASICS: WHAT IT TAKES TO QUALIFY — 81

What Kind of House Can You Afford? — 84
What Interest Rate Will You Pay? — 85

CLOSING COUNTDOWN: EXERCISING YOUR OPTION TO PURCHASE — 87

Lessons Learned in Hindsight — 89

CROSSING THE FINISH LINE: MARIA'S INSPIRATIONAL STORY — 91

GLOSSARY OF TERMS — 95

Table of Contents

FOREWORD	**V**
INTRODUCTION	**1**
Why Did We Write this Guide?	2
How You Can Get the Most Out of this Guide	3
UNDERSTANDING RENT TO OWN	**5**
Tired of Paying Down Your Landlord's Mortgage?	6
Who is the Typical Rent to Own Homebuyer?	6
Are You Investment-Minded?	7
PUT YOUR 'INVESTOR HAT' ON	**11**
Why is Buying Better than Renting?	12
Buying Helps You Harness the Power of "Leverage"	13
Buying Allows You to Earn Extra Cash	14
Why Rent to Own?	14
Look at the Big Picture to Get Ahead	17
IS RENT TO OWN ALWAYS THE WAY?	**19**
Is Homeownership Really Your Biggest Goal?	19
High Interest Rate Mortgage vs. Rent to Own	20
7 Reasons You Can be Turned Down for a Mortgage	22
17 SMART REASONS TO RENT TO OWN	**27**
8 LITTLE FLAWS OF RENT TO OWN	**35**
TWO WAYS TO RENT TO OWN: WHICH IS RIGHT FOR YOU?	**41**
Scenario A: You Found a House You'd Love to Own	41
Scenario B: Qualify for Rent to Own First	43
Rent to Own an "Inventory" House	44
Which Type of Rent to Own is Best?	45

Foreword

I'll start by saying this Guide is a MUST-READ for anybody considering rent to own (RTO) as a homebuyer. It will describe in detail what to look for, how to protect your or your family's interests, what questions to ask, and the necessary detailed steps to take on the homebuyer side of a RTO transaction. Simply put, you'll get the straight goods showing the good, the bad, and the ugly.

When Neil and Rachel invited me to write the foreword to this guide I was both flattered and honored. They have helped countless families through the rent to own process and I respect how they do business and admire what they stand for; which is win-win for all parties. Too often nowadays used as a cliché, they actually execute that in word and deed ("walk the talk"). I have known them for several years now through the real estate circle of my industry. As a top producing Home Financing Advisor (mortgage specialist) for Scotiabank, a major bank in Canada, I work with everyone from first time buyers, move-up buyers, and seasoned investors. I come across many companies and self-proclaimed experts in the real estate field. Whether its realtors, investors, lenders, lawyers, builders, or rent to own companies, I never found a shortage of who to work with, yet Neil and Rachel always made a favourable impression.

In addition to my work as a mortgage specialist, I am also an active real estate investor. I have watched Neil and Rachel's endeavors evolve and grow for several years. So when it came time for me to expand my investment portfolio, I chose their rent to own opportunities to investigate. I always liked the RTO model as it seemed like a win-win for both the investor and the homebuyer. Unfortunately I learned the RTO model was not without its pitfalls (and unscrupulous companies or investors). However, I am very careful about who I trust. It took a detailed process for me to choose Neil and Rachel as the trusted guardians of my real estate investments as well as feeling comfortable enough to refer my own friends and family.

In my investment pursuits, I met rent to own companies that have offered me higher projected returns and a "rosier" depiction of the RTO reality than I expected. It also became clear that while trying to lure investors, other companies were not overly concerned about the homebuyers themselves; which in my mind was a recipe for disaster. What I liked about Neil and Rachel is that they were realistic and conservative in their projections and laid out the good, the bad, and the ugly. They were clear that their aim was to equally protect the interests of the investor and the homebuyer. As a mortgage professional I really appreciated that as I feel that too often today people are given what I call the "drive-through" answer. In the mortgage industry that looks like: "here's your interest rate, here's your payment, call me if you need anything." Well what about the countless scenarios that may arise due to life changes? What about all of the options you can have at your disposal? I'll elaborate what that means specifically in the RTO scenario.

As a mortgage specialist, my job is to qualify clients for the bank that I think are fit to receive financing and then explain to the bank why I think that is so. As an investor in the RTO model, my role changed to that of a "bank" or lender and Neil's job was to qualify the tenant buyer. Since I was very familiar with what a bank looks for when providing a mortgage, I was one of the people that Neil questioned thoroughly as to future mortgage qualification for his homebuyers. What impressed me most was his genuine concern for the people he was helping to become homeowners as he wanted to ensure that once their term as RTO tenants ended and it came time to qualify for a mortgage he was determined to leave no stone unturned. I felt he really wanted to protect their interests by asking me questions such as:

What percentage of their income is required to pay for shelter costs when qualifying vs. what is a safe recommended percentage that would leave a margin for error?

What is the minimum down payment required today? vs. What if that law changes in the future?

Will a bank recognize a Rent to own agreement as a legitimate structure and saving tool? What key elements must be present?

Will Canada's Mortgage Insurers (such as CMHC – Canada Mortgage Housing Corporation, or Genworth Financial) also recognize a RTO agreement as a legitimate structure and saving tool? What key elements must be present?

What types of income does the bank accept outside of traditional sources of employment? (ie. Spousal support, child tax benefits, basement rental income, self-employment guidelines, etc.)

How does the bank view bankruptcies, consumer proposals, and other blemishes on ones credit history? And more importantly what can the client do to bridge that gap?

Furthermore, he explained that he would facilitate annual consultation sessions with mortgage professionals to ensure that these families were on the right track. These are just some of the things we discussed to ensure that homebuyers would be ready to qualify for a mortgage when the time came.

As an investor now acting as a lender of sorts, I wanted to ensure the people Neil presented to me were credit worthy. So I examined everything. I started with their credit reports and asked the tough questions of why some blemishes took place while factoring in the human element of life changes. I meticulously reviewed employment documentation (job letters, pay stubs), any other relevant documents, and spent the time to call and verify those details. And finally, for my first couple of investments I chose to meet the homebuyers face to face (although many investors choose not to). I guess I'm traditional like that where I like to shake people's hands, look them in the eyes and feel them out. I call this my gut check.

This is the only part of this process that is unscientific to me but I like to trust my gut as it never let me down before and I urge you, the reader to do the same (but only after you've gone through the entire logical and necessary checklist of fact finding).

All the families in Neil and Rachel's program chose their houses and had the investor buy the house on their behalf. This last point seems obvious, however there are several RTO companies out there that suggest an investor buy a house and then try to fill it with a homebuyer; big mistake. When the tenant buyer chooses their home, it invariably creates a feeling of ownership from the start, not to mention that its typically an upgrade from a rental property where they've come from.

Although I obviously invest for profit, I believe in the RTO model as it allows me to make a real tangible difference in people's lives and help them get back on their feet. It wasn't long ago that I had financial woes. I know the anxiety feeling "being boxed in" can bring. That's why it gives me great pleasure to know that my investments have already helped several families such as (and I'll be brief for privacy reasons) a man who's been through a tragic accident, a newly married couple putting a bankruptcy behind them, a couple that was unfortunately swindled by an investor, and a newly formed family straightening out their lives from previous divorce.

As previously mentioned, this guide is a great starting point to get educated on the true process of rent to own and examine whether its affordability (on either side of the transaction) is the right option for you. Neil and Rachel have helped countless families in the RTO process, and what I can promise you, the reader, is that should you choose to proceed and get qualified, Neil and Rachel would treat you with the same care and diligence they have shown me and all the families that I've worked with.

Good luck and happy reading!
Michael Yosher
Home Financing Advisor, Scotiabank, Toronto, Canada

Introduction

Financial freedom.
Stable environment for our kids.
Peace of mind.
Happiness.

That's what we listed when writing down the main reasons we wanted to buy our first home. About 10 years ago, my husband and I made a decision to stop renting and start owning. Putting money into someone else's pocket was one of the biggest disadvantages we found about renting. But we didn't really understand how owning a home actually puts money into our own pocket until about three years later, when we needed to renew our mortgage. Our mortgage broker happily blurted out that we had $45,000 in equity! Apparently our house grew in value. Actually he said our home had appreciated by about four percent. Just by making regular mortgage payments, we made a decent dent in the amount we borrowed from the bank to buy the house in the first place. The difference between what we owed the bank and what our house's street value was at that time is how we managed to earn $45,000 in three years. If we were to sell our house at that time, we could pocket that money as profit. But since we were not ready to move, we decided to take the money out as equity and pay down some debt.

We obliterated credit card debt, line of credit debt and had enough to cover an all-inclusive vacation to the Dominican Republic. From this experience, we realized that owning real estate could help us achieve our long-term financial goals. It was only logical to use some of the equity we earned to buy another house. A real estate investor from the US turned us on to the idea of rent to own. So when our realtor introduced us to a young family who wanted to rent to own the house they were renting, we had to consider it. The concept was sound – anyone who has a blemished credit report and low down payment could use rent to own as a "tool" to get into homeownership, as long as they had a stable income and a commitment to improve their credit. In essence we could help people become homeowners while at the same time helping achieve some of our financial goals – a win-win.

The idea of renting to own a home was not very well known back in 2009 when we stumbled upon it and began educating ourselves. But it is now fast becoming a very viable "alternative financing" option. It is ideal for people who no longer want to throw their money away on rent but cannot get approved for a mortgage the traditional way. For us, it was simply a great way to help people.

One thing kept re-surfacing – mixed emotions from people who had heard of rent to own. So before jumping into rent to own, we did extensive research. Indeed there were stories circulating on the internet about how someone got scammed and that it doesn't work for the "average person". Closer investigation was needed. Our curiosity led us to interview other investors who were involved with rent to own. Unfortunately there was some truth to the gossip we found online. Nonetheless, we uncovered interesting information. After extensive deliberation, we were convinced we could help families rent to own a home in a way that would position them for success not set them back. So we set out to prove it.

In 2009 we created a rent to own program that is aimed at helping people become home owners at the end of a pre-determined rent to own period. Our mission is to educate families and individuals about the realities of rent to own so they can be empowered to succeed. Through open and honest information sharing, we hope to increase the success rate of people who choose to use the rent to own path to homeownership. Our program is designed to make renting to own a positive experience for both the people who will become the homebuyers *and* the investor that is helping them get there. We personally facilitated rent to own arrangements for over 50 families in our local area where we carefully matched families with investors who share our commitment to help people get ahead with rent to own. In 2009 we set out to educate homebuyers on how to rent to own and come out ahead. We have since counseled over 500 families, single professionals and people looking for a fresh start.

Why Did We Write this Guide?

Quite simply, we want to share the secrets of success and reassure skeptics that rent to own can be an excellent path to homeownership. The sincere, optimistic feedback we received from people we've counseled over the years has been inspirational. It is so exhilarating to see the positive impact a rent to own option can make in people's lives – especially for people who were not ready to give up and were ready to receive help. So when people ask us what is the "key to success" with rent to own, we can confidently say – an informed and proactive homebuyer. Since we go over this point often, it is in fact a key reason we decided to write this guide.

Our family-run rent to own program has helped over 50 families get a chance at a home they otherwise would not be able to buy. Each family selects a home they love, move in and treat it as their own until they can qualify for a traditional mortgage. While they live there, often they are working towards improving their credit and building up their down payment so that they can meet the lender's criteria by a set date.

Through this guide, we want to help more individuals and families determine if rent to own is the right choice. If it is, we have shared a lot of insights to help you succeed in a rent to own arrangement. As with anything, there is a lot of information floating out there – some of it misleading, some of it true. Life is busy. Pulling all the information together and making sense of it all can be challenging and time consuming. In this guide we give you an insider's scoop on the pros and cons involved in renting to own a home. Renting to own, just like homeownership is a big commitment. Our hope is that this guide will give you a better understanding of what rent to own can offer you so that you are able to make an educated decision whether it is a good fit for you and your family.

How You Can Get the Most Out of this Guide

We encourage you to read this guide from start to finish. That way you are sure to learn what you need to know and get answers to most (hopefully all) of your questions. And if you still have unanswered questions, reach out to us at info@renting2own.ca.

To help you anticipate what stumps most people, we included many "HOMEBUYER BEWARE TIPs" throughout this guide. These tips are easy to spot and can help educate you about how to avoid costly pitfalls that may cross your path. We admit that some of the terminology we use throughout the guide may be intimidating because it is unfamiliar. To help you wrap your head around some of new ideas we present, we included a glossary at the back of the guide. While you're there, check out the worksheets. We wanted to give you a head start on achieving your homeownership goals – whether you choose the rent to own path or not, these worksheets can be a good springboard. Ultimately, the information in this guide is aimed at helping you keep your finances safe and on track to successfully achieving your goal of becoming a homeowner.

In the chapters that follow, you will learn what rent to own is and how it works, you'll also discover the different ways a rent to own can be done – along with the benefits and disadvantages of each approach. Just like not everyone can qualify for a mortgage today, not everyone is ready to get into a rent to own situation. We'll explain who has the best shot of actually getting ahead with rent to own. One of our favourite chapters is the where we reveal the pros and cons of renting to own a home. We have even included a chart that summarizes what a reasonable rent to own agreement may contain. If you decide that rent to own is the right option for you, then be sure to read Chapter 11 (*The 18 Rules of Success*). We share important insights from the trenches to help you take ownership end up with money in _your_ pocket.

It is our sincere hope that sharing our experience will help you get into the right rent to own arrangement if you cannot qualify for a mortgage today. Just by reading the stories of other families' experiences with rent to own, you are miles ahead of most people considering this path. Armed with important knowledge we share here, you are likelier to be successful if you choose to rent to own. Congratulations on making a smart first step.

IMPORTANT NOTE: We offer this guide as a self-help tool for educational purposes. Since we live and work in Canada, much of the information (and spelling) has a Canadian slant. All the more reason to take the information we share and use it to fuel your discussions with professionals in your area. The valuable insights you gain from this guide should supplement rather than replace professional financial, mortgage, real estate or legal advice. We have made every effort to provide realistic examples and share real numbers. Please remember, all calculations are examples only. We cannot guarantee that the information in this guide will apply or help your particular situation.

CHAPTER 1

Understanding Rent to Own

Simply put, rent to own is a stepping-stone for renters who dream of owning their own home. The idea of getting into homeownership via rent to own is not brand new. Also known as "lease-to-own", "lease option" or "lease purchase homes", it is a concept whose time has come. With lending rules getting tighter and tighter, it is rapidly growing in popularity across Canada, USA and Europe.

Rent to own is fast becoming a very viable "alternative financing" option for people who have decided that they no longer want to throw their money away on rent and want to own their own home even though they could not get approved for a mortgage the traditional way. The families we've helped over the years have certainly validated that rent to own can be a sound alternative to get into homeownership even when lenders turn you down for a mortgage.

Historically, rent to own was a legally documented transaction under which consumer goods (furniture, electronics) were leased in exchange for a weekly or monthly payment. The people were comfortable paying for the privilege of using certain merchandise, like a TV, if they were unable to pay for it outright. Anyone leasing merchandise had the option to purchase at some point during the agreement or return the merchandise. When renting to own merchandise, the lessee is not obligated to purchase since the agreement can be terminated at any point with the return of the merchandise.

Having the option to rent to own a home is not a new concept either. Some Canadians were doing it as far back as the 70's in different forms. However, the current economic conditions in the United States are helping to popularize the rent to own approach to homeownership. Many Americans have been affected by the sinking economy, whether it's stock market declines, job layoffs, foreclosures, or bankruptcies, the impact has led some people to change the "traditional" way they had lived their lives. Many Americans lost their homes or are on the verge of losing them because they cannot afford their monthly payments anymore. Also many current homeowners have seen their credit scores badly damaged. Which means there's little hope of re-financing or getting another mortgage until they successfully improve their credit or find a way to save up a larger down payment than was accepted in the past. Canadians have also felt the pinch as government regulations were recently altered, making it harder for the average Canadian to qualify for a mortgage.

Tired of Paying Down Your Landlord's Mortgage?

If you have been renting, I am sure you can look back at your rent payments and start adding up how much money you have given to your landlord to pay down *their* mortgage. For example, if you have been renting for three years at the same location and have been paying $1,400 a month, $54,400 is what you would have spent on rent. What that really means is that you gave your landlord $54,400 to pay down their mortgage. Ouch. While there are merits to renting (especially if you move frequently), it makes less sense if you plan to put down roots in one location. Think about it, owning a home gives you stability and freedom to do things your way. Plus you have the added benefit of building equity as your home goes up in value year over year. If low down payment or poor credit stand in the way of you getting into homeownership, rent to own can be a good solution. Rent to own can help you stop renting and start owning when the banks turn you down.

Who is the Typical Rent to Own Homebuyer?

Rent to own is for people who can improve their credit and build up a down payment in three or four years time. It is ideal for people who want to stop renting but need time to repair bruised credit or save a bigger down payment to qualify for their own mortgage. In it's truest form, a rent to own is an arrangement between an investor who is on title of the home that a family or individual (homebuyer) wants to purchase from the investor at the end of a pre-determined rental period. The arrangement typically involves both parties agreeing on the future purchase price of the home, and the date the homebuyer will purchase it. In other words, the ideal homebuyer is someone who can afford the home and intends to qualify for a mortgage by a specific date in the future in order to take ownership of the house in their name.

If the homebuyer is proactive and uses the rental period wisely, they will be able to improve their credit situation or down payment situation or both, in order to meet the lenders' criteria so they can qualify for their own mortgage.

The length of a rent to own arrangement can run anywhere from one to five years – depending how much time the homebuyer needs to improve their credit or save up for a down payment. For the duration of the rent to own period, the homebuyer makes a monthly payment to the investor. Usually, a portion of the homebuyer's monthly payment is "credited" back to the homebuyer and the accumulated credit comes off of the agreed upon purchase price. This essentially is where your down payment comes from.

Typically, a homebuyer could expect to pay slightly more each month for the right to enter into this arrangement, but it is more like putting money back in your pocket over time. For example, if a house would typically rent for $1,200, you might be asked to pay $1,500 per month. The good news is that -- $300 -- would be credited toward your down payment. Over three years, you could accumulate $10,800 toward your down payment. The key is to qualify for a mortgage and exercise your option to purchase the home by the end of the rent to own term to be able to use the down payment credit you accumulated.

Before you start thinking: *I can put aside $300 a month, why would I need a rent to own* – allow us to clarify. Rent to own is more than just saving money each month towards a down payment. In a rent to own, you are also building equity during your rental period – and that puts money back in your pocket. We'll discuss those perks in more detail in Chapter 4 (*16 Smart Reasons to Rent to Own*).

Did you know your down payment can be an important component in determining the price of the house you can afford and the type of lending terms you get when applying for a traditional mortgage? Most traditional lenders will consider giving a mortgage to someone with stellar credit and a five percent down payment. However, if your credit is tarnished, a traditional lender may want 10-15 percent down. Rent to own can be more forgiving. Although you don't need a large down payment for rent to own, you do need to have some money to put down initially (often in lieu of first and last month's rent). You may qualify for rent to own with a 2.5 or 5 percent down, despite your tarnished credit. Our rent to own program is structured in such a way that you can add to your initial down payment and accumulate a 10 percent down payment by the end of the term. Although it may sound like a good idea to get into a rent to own arrangement with as little down as possible, the size of your down payment is critical in determining your monthly payments, and ultimately what you can afford to buy. The more you put down initially, the lower your monthly rent to own payment, and the more affordable the future purchase.

Are You Investment-Minded?

Believe it or not, the lines are starting to blur as to whom the perfect rent to own candidate is. More and more we see rent to own attracting investment-minded folks who use leverage to generate a profit from residential real estate. Although they may have the 10 percent for the down payment the banks want, they prefer a rent to own arrangement because they can tie up less of their own capital in the house. A rent to own arrangement allows them to put down three to five percent to get the house they want to start building equity in – all without tying up additional funds on the purchase. Smart.

In a nutshell, a well-planned rent to own arrangement gives you access to equity and buys you time. Time to establish or repair your credit and time to save or add to your down payment. Monique and Al experienced this first hand.

A married couple in their early thirties, Monique and Al started renting a cozy one bedroom basement apartment in Barrie, Ontario shortly after their wedding three years earlier. The rent was low and allowed them to put money away so they could buy a house down the road.

Both were employed full-time, Monique as a nurse and Al as a mechanic. With better than average incomes, the couple was building up a decent nest egg. Everything was going as planned until Monique got pregnant and had to take maternity leave. Although she received a top-up from her employer while off, it was a far cry from her regular pay cheque. The couple started to feel the pinch. The birth of their first child was one of the most joyful experiences of their lives, but four months later Al lost his job. This put a significant strain on them financially and they had to really dip into their savings to stay on top of their expenses. For five months Al was unable to secure new employment and their savings dried up. They were forced to use their credit cards to stay afloat. When Al finally did get work, it was part-time and the pay was hardly enough to get them back on track.

Although she would have liked to take a full year off with her baby, Monique returned to work when the baby was only nine months old to help keep their family afloat. Even though their financial issues had stabilized within a few months, they had incurred debt and became a credit concern due to missed and late payments. To top it off, the cozy one bedroom they were in had become far too crowded for the growing family.

Three months later, Monique and Al decided they wanted to start fresh. With about $6,000 in savings, they chose to make the move into their own home, which would also give them more space. Their real estate agent suggested they get pre-qualified for a mortgage to make the home search a bit more efficient. Two lenders turned them down because of Al's recent job loss and delinquent credit card payments. However one mortgage broker said he could help them. But Monique and Al would need between 15-20 percent down. In Barrie, Ontario the type of houses they wanted listed for about $250,000. That would mean the couple needed a down payment of about $37,500. With only $6,000 to their name and tarnished credit, getting a mortgage was not realistic. They needed more time to save.

Monique was telling a colleague at the hospital about her disappointing mortgage situation. That's when she heard about rent to own for the first time. The couple did their research to make sure rent to own was truly a better option than renting and putting money aside on their own to build up their down payment.

Even though the couple was good at saving, Monique knew they would end up with a higher down payment with the customized rent to own program they were considering. Plus she recognized they can use some support to improve their credit scores in time to qualify for a mortgage. The biggest deciding factor for Monique was the chance to move in right away and enjoy the extra space and have the freedom to decorate the baby's room at last. In three short years Monique and Al saw themselves actually qualifying for a mortgage when they go apply. For the first time since their troubles started, they could see the light at the end of a tunnel.

Monique and Al found a three-bedroom home that they loved in Barrie, Ontario, Canada. The house offered a lot of room for storage and a spacious backyard for their growing son to run around. The couple is getting support to fix their credit and at the end of the three-year rent to own term they will have about $28,000 towards their down payment for this house.

If Monique and Al continued to rent for another three years, they would have spent about $43,000 paying off their landlord's mortgage, instead of getting closer to putting money back in their pocket to get back on track with their finances. As an average, think about this situation:

You have been renting for four years. It appears to be a logical step due to the convenience of being able to move without the hassles of selling a house and purchasing a new one. But is convenience enough? Ironically, most people who think that they will require the "convenience" because they plan to move more often actually stay in the same location far longer than they think. Let's look at it in financial terms. Over the four years that you are renting, you pay an average of $1,600 a month to your landlord for the privilege of living in their house. Multiply $1,600 by 48 months (four years) and you have just paid your landlord $76,800! The math is easy to do but at the same time, it is scary to see the results. So most people avoid the math all together. Now what happens if your landlord comes to you and says that he/she wants to move back in to the house or sell it? How much of that $76,800 will you get back? You already know the answer so we don't really need to push this any further.

Lets turn the tables on this example and consider that if you had put that same $76,800 into your own house over the same time (own outright or rent to own), you could potentially see much of this money come back to you if you were to refinance and take out equity or sell and move on. It certainly doesn't take much calculation to see which situation could benefit you more in the future. Sure, there are expenses associated with homeownership – repairs, maintenance, etc. But in reality, if you have done your due diligence, completed a home inspection and were dedicated to the general upkeep of the property, those costs will be far less than the money you would have doled out while renting.

Like Monique and Al, many people who want to own their own house have found their path blocked by one or more personal circumstances. Often they consider only the most common option: rent until you can buy. However, rent to own, is another option. It combines some of the advantages of renting with many of the benefits of ownership. Rent to own can offer you the break you need to start owning sooner than you may have thought possible.

Remember to use the **HOMEBUYER BEWARE TIPs** throughout this guide. They are intended to flag pitfalls at a glance, prompt you to take action and protect yourself. Take these tips seriously and keep re-reading them if you want to succeed going the rent to own way.

HOMEBUYER BEWARE TIP

Mortgage lending criteria may change in the coming years. If you are working towards only a 5 per cent down payment through your rent to own term, it may not be enough. What if lenders insist on a minimum down payment of 10 percent when you apply? If this is the case, you may want to use the rent to own term to save a significantly higher amount toward your down payment.

CHAPTER 2

Put Your 'Investor Hat' On

To some, a house is just a home, not an investment. When these folks think about owning a home, they envision a backyard for kids to play in, a bright kitchen where family gathers, a cozy finished basement with rec room, the kids' school around the corner, easy access to work and shopping within a ten-minute drive. This way of thinking about your house can certainly pay off, mostly in a non-financial way, through the enjoyment of the house.

What if your rent to own arrangement was also a moneymaking opportunity for you? Consider for a moment that your house is an investment for your future. If historical data tells us anything, it's that most properties increase in value year over year. Sure, there is always the chance of a dip due to market conditions but if you look at the value of most houses over a 20-year stretch, you can bet that the house values have seen more increases than dips. What does that mean to you? Well, by the time you are ready to retire, the house should be worth a whole lot more than what you paid for it and you can enjoy some security in your retirement years. Who wants to be working into their sixties to pay the rent?

In actuality, houses in Canada have grown in value on average, about 5.4 percent each year since 1980.[1] Metropolitan cities like Toronto and Vancouver are particularly popular among people seeking a cultured, dynamic lifestyle. For this reason property values in these cities will likely continue to see good growth. In Toronto for example, homeowners have enjoyed 6.1 percent on average between 1980 and 2012. Homeowners in Vancouver did slightly better with 6.4 percent return on investment.[2]

Let's put things into perspective. If you purchased a house in Toronto in 1988 for about $95,000, on average, it would have grown in value by 5.4 percent each year. Fast forward to 2013. Your house is worth almost $371,000 and you no longer have mortgage payments. What you do have is piece of mind that your house is paid for.

---

[1] Source: http://business.financialpost.com, *"TD: House Prices to Remain Flat for 10 Years"*
[2] Source: http://www.thestar.com, *"Canadian Housing Prices to rise lackluster 2 per year: TD"*

Calculating Future Value of a House	
Home's Starting Value	$95,000
Number of Years Owned	25
Estimated Annual Appreciation Rate	5.60%
Estimated Home Value Today	**$370,995**

Note: Appreciation rates vary from year to year. This calculation is for illustration purposes only. It is not intended to predict appreciation values and is not a promise of future appreciation. Please consult a mortgage professional or a realtor for more concrete information.

If your house is in a high-demand metropolitan area like Toronto or Vancouver, your home's value in 25 years could be substantially higher because of more favourable appreciation. Consider this true story:

"My mom has a grade 4 education and bought a house back in 1980 in the middle of downtown Toronto for 50,000 dollars. It's worth close to 700,000 dollars now. She had no clue houses could appreciate, in fact, she had no idea what appreciation was. Heck, she has no idea what a stock is and how to buy it. We rented out all 7 rooms to pay off the mortgage in 5 years time. What do you know, we still live here and my mom, who made only minimum wage all her life is a millionaire!!! She stopped working at age 49!" [3]

Why is Buying Better than Renting?

Some people will challenge that homeownership can cost more because you have to borrow money and pay property taxes, maintenance and so on. We would argue that as a renter you are already paying for all these expenses and then some. In reality, your landlord includes these expenses in the monthly rent. Those expenses are not the only thing you're paying. The landlord typically wants to make a profit on the property that you are renting. So your rent is actually comprised of the landlord's profit and expenses. If the property requires any repairs, to cut costs, a landlord may take shortcuts, delay doing the work or decline to do it all together. Out of frustration, many renters take matters into their own hands and simply pay for the repairs out of pocket. If they are dealing with a reasonable landlord, you can negotiate to have the expenses reimbursed or subtracted from the rent owing. In reality, there are many renters who simply absorb the costs. Either way, this unneeded aggravation (and expense) is enough to make many renters wish they owned their own place. The bottom line is that if you are renting, don't think for a minute that

---

[3] Source: http://business.financialpost.com, *"Why its Better To Rent than Buy"*

you are not paying property taxes, interest on mortgage or property maintenance fees. They are probably hidden in your rent! Plus when you move out, you have nothing to show for it.

If you stop paying the landlord's mortgage and start paying your own, after 25 years you'll likely eliminate your monthly payments and still end up with a roof over your head. If you remain a renter, you probably won't have the same luxury. Where will you end up? Still working well into your retirement years so that you can pay the rent. Good thing Wal-Mart is always hiring.

From a financial standpoint, experts will tell you that it makes sense to invest in a home when you have the down payment and your interest rate does not exceed 5 percent. Ultimately, it comes down to whether you can afford the house you want and whether you can qualify for a mortgage. If you can't qualify today, rent to own is a viable option to get you on the path to homeownership sooner. A good rent to own company should be able to help you determine what kind of home you can afford and how much you need to pay each month to accumulate the necessary down payment. It is also a good idea to speak with a mortgage broker to get a second opinion. They can advise you on what you'll need to qualify for a mortgage and maybe even discuss where mortgage interest rates are headed.

Buying Helps You Harness the Power of "Leverage"

Considering whether your house will have good appreciation is an important aspect of having an investor mindset when it comes to selecting a house to rent to own. But it is not the only consideration. We cannot ignore the importance of leverage. It is critical for you as a potential homeowner to grasp how leverage works in housing. In a rent to own, you can put down around 2.3 percent or $6,500 on a $280,000 house. Your future purchase price after three years may be around $320,000. Let's say you are handy and spend about $3,500 improving the kitchen over three years. The value of the house will likely go up. For example, if the property value jumps to $340,000 at the end of a three-year rent to own program, you've made a nice profit. Effectively, you used your initial down payment of $6,500 to generate $20,000 in equity – subtract your renovation costs and initial down payment and you can pocket a $10,000 profit. The best part is that you used the investor's money as leverage to double the cash you put in. If you think like an investor when considering a rent to own arrangement, you may uncover an opportunity to earn a 100 percent return on your investment. Now, we are not suggesting that you can go from renting to own a house to being a real estate tycoon by leveraging other people's money or credit. There is much more to know about how to make money in residential real estate. What we are trying to illustrate is that you should look at your rent to own home as an opportunity to grow the money you put into it, as much as you look at it as a roof over your head.

Buying Allows You to Earn Extra Cash

In the spirit of entering a rent to own arrangement with an investor mindset, you can also consider renting out your house. After the rent to own term is finished, or a few years later many homebuyers opt to sell and acquire something bigger. Instead of selling, you can rent out the house so that your renters cover your mortgage and expenses, while you continue to build equity. Did you know you can rent out a $250,000 house in most parts of Canada for $1,600 per month or more? If your carrying costs (property taxes, interest, insurance) are around $1,300 per month, you can actually benefit from $300 a month in cash flow and possibly net a profit close to $3,600 at the end of the year. Remember, this option is available to you once you take ownership of your rent to own property.

Why Rent to Own?

Appreciation. Appreciation. Appreciation. It is a fact that the actual structural quality of a house will slowly decrease over time, but it is important to know that the market value of a well-maintained house will increase (or appreciate) over time.

Safeguard your investment by understanding how your appreciation will be calculated. The single most important question you need to ask: *what appreciation rate was used to calculate your future purchase price.*

Many rent to own companies charge a standard, across the board appreciation rate. Often the appreciation rate is inflated. Is this fair? Most likely not, since not all neighbourhoods are created equal. In the context of your rent to own arrangement, an inflated appreciation rate may cause your future purchase price to be inflated as well. At the end of the rent to own term when you apply for a mortgage, the bank will likely request an appraisal. If your future purchase price was based on fair appreciation value, your chances are much higher of getting approved for a mortgage (provided your application meets other important lender criteria we discuss in chapter 12).

HOMEBUYER BEWARE TIP

Be sure to ask how the appreciation rate is calculated, you deserve to know before you commit to a rent to own arrangement. If the appraisal comes in much lower than the future purchase price you locked into, you may not be able to get your mortgage. In this case, you will either have to walk away from the house or come up with more money on short notice.

While it may be challenging to judge whether the appreciation rate you are given is reasonable, remember Canadian example? Houses here have grown in value about 5.4 percent each year since 1980.[4] Unless you are renting to own a house in downtown Toronto or Vancouver, the appreciation rate should be lower than the national average. If you're considering doing a rent to own in the US, establishing fair appreciation rates may be a bit more difficult, given that the housing market is still recovering. According to one study, house prices in the USA rose by more than 5 percent between from 2012 to 2013. The data the data also suggests places like Oakland, San Jose and even Detroit have had home price increases of well more than 25 percent. Speak with local realtors and mortgage professionals to help you determine what fair appreciation averages may be in your area.[5]

Beyond that question, you should have a good idea of the other factors that can affect appreciation rates. Be sure to understand how the area, neighborhood, and market have been appreciating historically. If you aren't sure how to do this, speak with your realtor or a rent to own company. Here are some things you can look for to determine if the appreciation rate is fair.

CHECK RECENT SALES

Do a comparative market analysis or view the public records at the tax assessors' office. This should give you a feel for the amount of sales in the area, the direction of the sale prices and whether or not the houses are selling for more than the list price (which is a hot button for appreciation).

TRACK THE TRENDS

Follow real estate trends in the area and be sure to stay on top of the local business news. Is there something major coming into the area? Find out what it will be. Many times this will bring more people to the area and increase demand. On the flip side though, the type of industry can also have a negative impact especially if it is not overly desirable (think garbage dump). You can usually get much of this information at the office for planning and development in the area you want to live in.

---

[4] Source: http://business.financialpost.com, *"TD: Canadian Home Prices to be Flat for Next 10 Years"*

[5] Source: http://finance.yahoo.com, *"America's Hottest Housing Markets"*

Rent to Own Essential Guide for Homebuyers

ANALYZE THE NEIGHBOURHOOD

Get to know the neighborhood and what the history for the area looks like. Have the prices in the area increased in value historically, bounced back and forth or have they remained stable? Is it a desirable area? Affordable? Are there great schools and amenities close by? What about transit? All of these factors will play a role in determining how desirable the area is or will be in the future.

UNCOVER DEVELOPMENT PLANS

Development in the area can be a two-edged sword depending on the type of development. Malls, transit and other amenities can have a positive impact on the value of your home. When your house is close to amenities, the value of the house can go up faster. On the other hand, the development of more housing in your area could have a negative impact as it will increase the supply of homes in the area. There are those that argue, however, that new housing construction can also boost the values in the area because new houses typically come with a higher price tag.

The bottom line is that you should focus on buying a reasonably priced home in a stable and desirable neighborhood. If you are eager to boost the home's value faster, invest in home improvements that add value. These include kitchen upgrades, bathroom upgrades, finishing the basement, etc. You are more than likely to reap the financial benefits at the end of the rent to own term. In many cases, you are likely to see a profit in the form of equity.

A fresh coat of paint on the outside of your house goes a long way. Not only does it help to increase property value, it also boosts a home's appeal. You can go a step further to give your freshly painted house even more pizzazz. Simply trim overgrown shrubs and plant bright coloured flowers.

Familiarize yourself with the various factors that help increase the appreciation rate of your home. This knowledge can help you determine what can influence your ability to build equity and generate a profit in the future.

Jeff and Joanne from Bradenton, Florida bought a modest house that had potential. The exterior of the house was peeling and there were several patches with mildew stains. They took time off work and re-painted all sides of the house. Their sweat equity paid off. Over $7,000 in equity went into their pocket at the end of their rent to own term.

Look at the Big Picture to Get Ahead

If you choose to buy a house using the rent to own path, look at the bigger picture. Put your investor hat on when you are considering various houses. Choose a house whose value will rise if market conditions are good. In the long run, one of your goals should be to own a home that will be worth more than you paid for it. If you sell, you will make money. If you choose to live in it or rent it out, you will build equity. Either way you win. If you cannot get into homeownership on your own, rent to own gives you a sound way to leverage someone's money (and credit rating) to put you in a better position to build equity or generate a profit from your house. Ultimately a rent to own arrangement is an opportunity to get ahead financially, if that's what you want it to be.

CHAPTER 3

Is Rent to Own Always the Way?

Rent to own works in many different scenarios for many different people. Generally, rent to own is best suited for motivated people who are unable to qualify for a traditional mortgage at the present time but are not far from meeting the lender's criteria. People with no credit history or a lower credit score can be a good fit for rent to own as well. Anyone coming out of a divorce, consumer proposal or bankruptcy can benefit from rent to own because it offers time to build, repair or re-establish credit history. It can also work for people who may have over-extended an existing mortgage (first, second or third mortgage) and need to refinance. People in this situation can leverage rent to own in two ways to save their credit and their home. They can give up equity in the home in lieu of a down payment and rent to own their current home until they have sufficient funds and good credit to qualify for a mortgage. Alternatively, they can sell their current home, pay off the mortgage and use whatever is left as a down payment to rent to own another (more affordable) house.

On the other hand, rent to own may not the best approach for someone who does not have a stable employment income and an initial down payment. In particular, people on social assistance may find it difficult to meet rent to own obligations or lender criteria at the end of the rent to own term. In this case a conversation with a mortgage broker is highly recommended to determine the likelihood of getting a mortgage at the end of the rent to own term.

Now let's take a closer look at the many situations where rent to own can make sense.

Is Homeownership Really Your Biggest Goal?

First things first. Be honest with yourself. Unfortunately, it is not enough to say: *"I want to rent to own a home"*. You need to get more specific than that. Owning a home has to be your biggest goal. Goal setting is a powerful process for thinking about your ideal future, and for motivating yourself to turn your vision of this future into reality. After all, would you set out on a major journey with no real idea of your destination? Probably not. You would likely research your destination, the route, transportation options, associated costs and what to expect when you get there. Rent to own is not that different from that major journey we just mentioned.

Remember our couple back in Chapter 1, Monique and Al? This determined couple had dreams of homeownership and although they could not qualify for their own mortgage, they found that rent to own was a very real option that could help them build up their credit score and a down payment. Today, Monique and Al have qualified for their own mortgage and currently own their own home. Financially, they have never been in a better position and are building equity so they can finish their basement and generate rental income.

Setting your goals is actually easier than you might think. First you create your "big picture" goal. What do you want to get out of a rent to own arrangement? If you answer "homeownership" every time, rent to own might make sense for you.

Once you have your big picture goal defined, break your goal down into smaller targets that you must hit in order to reach your goal of homeownership. Throughout this Guide we caution you that just by being in a rent to own arrangement, you are not guaranteed to get qualified for a mortgage. When you are in a rent to own, consider the smaller targets you may need to hit to achieve your goal:

- Make monthly rent to own payments on time
- Pay down debt (consolidate if possible)
- Pay your bills on time without fail
- Understand your credit issues and work on improving your credit score
- Save a specific amount toward the down payment (as determined by your mortgage professional)
- Consult with a mortgage professional each year to ensure you're on track to qualify for a mortgage

The process of setting goals and establishing smaller targets also helps you determine what type of home you want. By knowing precisely what you want to end up with, you know where you have to concentrate your efforts to get there. You'll also quickly spot the distractions and poor fitting opportunities that can, so easily, lead you astray.

High Interest Rate Mortgage vs. Rent to Own

Typically, when you decide you want to own a home, you should speak to a lender, even if you know there's no chance you will qualify for a traditional mortgage today. Set up a face-to-face meeting with a mortgage specialist at a brokerage or at your local bank. When discussing "rough" numbers about your finances, be honest. That's the best way to find out what it will take for you to qualify for a mortgage.

If you do get approved for a mortgage, consider the interest rate you are being offered. With past credit issues and a lower down payment (between 5 and 10 percent), the interest rate you're offered may be considerably higher than the standard rates. A higher interest rate can drive up both your monthly payments and your cost of borrowing. If you've been approved for a mortgage and feel your interest rate is too high, investigate rent to own.

HOMEBUYER BEWARE TIP

Lenders may offer you a higher interest rate on your mortgage if you have a poor credit history along with a low down payment. This will result in higher monthly payments and higher costs of borrowing. Ask what the lowest rate is for someone with better credit or higher down payment and compare the cost of borrowing on the lowest rate and the rate you are being offered. Your rent to own payments may be more manageable than the high-interest mortgage.

If the mortgage professionals offer you an outrageous rate or simply cannot approve you for a mortgage today, rent to own might make sense for your situation. Rent to own still allows you to build equity during the rental period, so it is better than simply renting the next three years. Plus your rent to own monthly payment may be lower than your monthly high-interest mortgage payments. The best part is that you can build equity while building up a higher down payment or repairing your credit (or both). Talk about multi-tasking!

In a few short years you should have a bigger down payment and better credit score. That way the next time you meet with the mortgage broker or apply for a mortgage, you should qualify for a more favourable interest rate. A more favourable rate ultimately means you will save money on your monthly payments (provided your credit situation improved and you maintained a stable income).

HOMEBUYER BEWARE TIP

If you have poor credit, lenders may ask that you come in with as much as 20 percent down in order to qualify for a mortgage. For example, if you are interested in buying a $250,000 house, that means you'll need to put down $50,000 (20 percent) to get a mortgage. If you think you can afford the down payment, be sure to shop around for the best mortgage rate. To help you run the numbers, use online mortgage calculators like these ones:

YAHOO: http://homes.yahoo.com/calculators/amortization.html

CNN MONEY: http://cgi.money.cnn.com/tools/houseafford/houseafford.html

If you're in Canada and own an iPhone or iPad, check out this free mortgage calculator app:
https://itunes.apple.com/ca/app/canadian-mortgage/id509978685?mt=8

---

7 Reasons You Can be Turned Down for a Mortgage

You are not alone if you feel like renting is your only option! As mortgage rules tighten here in Canada, more and more people are finding it harder to get qualified for a mortgage from a traditional lender. Here we summarize which circumstances force lenders to turn you down for a mortgage.

#1 DIVORCE

The extreme financial impact of divorce can present challenges that can force you to re-organize you life in order to get back on your feet financially. In fact, one third of all bankruptcies are a result of separation or divorce. Why? Well, this occurs because expenses double while the individual incomes of the estranged husband and wife remain the same. The couple no longer shares the cost of living, making it harder to keep up with their respective monthly bills or stay on top of money owing on credit cards or other debt. Add child support or alimony payments into the mix, and it is easy to see why divorce can cause financial strain. Divorce can take a toll not just on the kids, but also on your bank account and credit history. Take Brynn for example.

Brynn had worked hard to improve her financial situation after a challenging divorce. She was tired of renting and had decided it was time to start putting her money towards something that mattered for her. She was confident that she could get a loan with 5 percent down. So she went to her bank in Oshawa, Ontario to get pre-approved for a mortgage before the realtor took her out to view houses. Brynn was clever to get the toughest question out of the way, right away – can I qualify for a mortgage?

To her surprise, the bank where Brynn held a savings account, chequing account and credit cards for many years started to scrutinize her "4 C's". They looked at her credit history, debt capacity and collateral. They verified her income for the past two years and they tried to predict how likely she was to keep her job. In other words, the bank was evaluating how stable Brynn's income was.

Unfortunately for Brynn, the news from the bank was devastating. Her application for a loan was declined. The bank explained that her credit rating was bruised during her divorce. Her recent job loss didn't help. The bills were not getting paid quickly enough and her debt was mounting. This was dragging down her finances and credit. The bank told her to try again in a couple of years. Brynn thought her only option was to continue renting.

"I thought I had a good marriage, unfortunately, not everything is as it seems. On top of that, I was employed by the same company for many years and was doing well in my position until I became a victim of a company restructuring which eliminated my position. It had been three years since the divorce and job loss and I thought I was really on my feet again, until the bank turned my application down," recalled Brynn.

Brynn went to friends for advice on how to buy her next home. A private mortgage was not an option as she did not want to get sucked into paying interest rates in excess of 12 percent on the loaned money. Fortunately, Brynn decided to pick up the phone and call a friend she had not spoken to since the divorce. "I was not sure what prompted the call but something inside me told me that I needed to speak to her," Brynn explained. Her friend mentioned she and her husband entered into a rent to own contract. She suggested it could fit Brynn's circumstances perfectly.

Rent to own helps divorcees like Brynn make a start fresh in a home they want to own. It affords time to repair credit and re-build finances so that a mortgage approval is achievable in a few short years. In many ways, Brynn is the ideal candidate for rent to own. She really wants the freedom of owning her own home. She has a stable income, a decent down payment and the drive to work on improving her credit situation. If you have similar circumstances, rent to own will likely make sense for you too.

HOMEBUYER BEWARE TIP

Always find out if you can qualify for a mortgage on your own before you pursue alternatives like rent to own or private lending. Compare the traditional lending terms with rent to own terms to determine which will cost you less in the next few years. A good accountant can help you crunch the numbers if you're not a "numbers person".

#2 NO CREDIT HISTORY

When considering giving you a mortgage, lenders want to know that you can pay them back. They rely heavily on your credit history to give them some clue about your credit-worthiness. Recent graduates from college or university who never owned a credit card may not be able to get a mortgage. New immigrants also have the same constraint. Lenders may not talk to you until you have established credit. Establishing credit is a very important step in getting approved for many types of loans, not just a mortgage. Take Jerrick and Freya from Australia, for example.

New to Canada because Jerrick was transferred here for his job, the couple started looking at buying a house. Unfortunately, no one told them they would need to have established credit before they could qualify for a mortgage. Jerrick and Freya had no choice but to rent.

The search for a rental took much longer than expected. They were finding properties that were too small, too expensive or needed lots of work just to make the house meet their standards. In the meantime, they still needed a roof over their head so they negotiated a short-term rental with a motel. Although the price was right, the location was seedy and their desire to get into something better was starting to take a toll on the couple. Jerrick was quite internet savvy so he started to search for alternatives to their current situation. During his search, he stumbled upon one of our ads that said no credit was required to rent to own a house. Curious if this was something that could work for them, Jerrick called us.

During a face-to-face meeting, Jerrick and Freya learned about our rent to own program and were assured that they could get the help they needed. They submitted their application and paperwork that verified their income. Based on that information they were approved for our rent to own program and could start shopping for a home. The couple told us the opportunity seemed too good to be true but felt comfortable enough with the information they received. Although it was hard for Jerrick and Freya to believe that they could pick their own house, they started the search. After only a few outings with the realtor, they found a house that had everything they needed. They had three percent to put down on the house. The monthly payments were higher than they anticipated, but still affordable, considering they were establishing their credit while living in their own home. They decided to go for it. Two years later, Jerrick and Freya are still in the rent to own program, and are one year away from qualifying for their own mortgage. By establishing a payment history through secured credit cards, they now have credit. Plus they grew their initial three percent down payment to almost 10 percent. To this day, Jerrick and Freya are very thankful they found our ad. Although homeownership presents new challenges for the couple (who will cut the grass!), they love the freedom of having a house they can treat as their own while they establish their credit scores.

Believe it or not, it may be that having bad credit is better than having no credit at all. Without credit, you have no credit history, no traceable payment history and no hope of getting qualified for a credit cards, car loan or mortgage. From the bank's perspective, if you have bad credit, you can still be classified.

Your credit report tells a story about you, regardless of whether or not the story is good or bad. The same cannot be said about people with no credit history, as there is no story on them. New immigrants, students and people who have found their way off of the credit grid are usually the best examples of people who can benefit from rent to own. A rent to own program not only gave Jerrick and Freya, new comers to Canada, a chance to move into a home they wanted to own sooner, it also gave them time to establish the credit they needed to get a mortgage for that house. If you have no credit history, a credible rent to own company can guide you to establish a credit rating. Chances are that you may be able to qualify for mortgage sooner than you think.

#3 PAST CREDIT PROBLEMS

Bad things can happen to good people. It is very possible that you ran into tough times in the past and had to "miss", "defer" or "default" on payments to stay afloat. Some people fall deep enough into debt trouble that they have to file for bankruptcy or consumer proposal. Fortunately credit is one of those things that can be repaired with a little time and focus while you are enjoying the house you will soon own.

 To help jumpstart you credit rehabilitation process check out the Credit Repair Worksheet included in the bonus gift pack you receive with purchase of this book. To claim your free gift pack email: info@renting2own.ca

4 SHORT EMPLOYMENT HISTORY

Nowadays, many lenders want to see a consistent employment track record. This usually means that they want to see at least one year and in many cases you need more than one year of history with a company. For people who are starting a new job or have been in a job for a short period of time, this makes it tough to get a mortgage. A rent to own offers these people the time required to establish a consistent track record of employment and earnings.

5 LOW DOWN PAYMENT

Unlike a traditional mortgage arrangement, in a rent to own, a small down payment is acceptable. For example, when you have less than perfect credit a lender may require you to have a minimum of 10 percent down in order to approve you for a mortgage at a reasonable rate. But what if you have only three percent? In a rent to own program, you can put that three percent down and add to it through your monthly payments over a specified period of time. In our rent to own program, homebuyers will typically accumulate a 10 percent down payment by the time they finish the rent to own program. On average, our homebuyers accumulate a $30,000 down payment within three years. A good rent to own arrangement should be structured in such a way that helps you accumulate a larger down payment over a certain period of time. Our homebuyers have often remarked that it is much easier to pay $400 a month towards their down payment while enjoying the house they want to own. Otherwise they'd be stuck paying down someone else's mortgage and struggling to save up a large amount like $30,000 before they can even think about house hunting.

6 SELF-EMPLOYED INCOME

It can be challenging for self-employed people to get approved for a mortgage. The tax benefits of owning your own business can lead many people to declare a nominal income for many years. If you are self-employed, chances are you can easily afford to buy a home and can even come up with a decent down payment. Unfortunately the income you claim on your tax return may tell lenders a different story. Lending institutions typically require at least two years of "Proof for Business Activity" and personal notice of assessments to determine what type of house you can purchase, and whether you're creditworthy for that particular house. If you want a bigger or more expensive house than lenders will agree to today, rent to own can be a great option. You can get the house you want today and get the time needed to establish a consistent income track record lenders want to see.

7 UNFORSEEN EVENTS TARNISHED YOUR CREDIT

If you or your family members have ever faced health issues or loss of a job, you know first hand how it can negatively impact your finances. If the issue is prolonged, it is not uncommon to fall behind on payments. Unfortunately, the credit bureau continues to track your bill-paying habits. It may not seem like much, but several months of missed or late payments can tarnish your credit. While these are usually temporary personal challenges, they can have a lasting impact on your credit history and interfere with you getting a mortgage. To get into a rent to own arrangement, your credit history does not need to be spotless. You can move into the house you want to own and take a few years to get your credit report back on track so that your mortgage application is well received by lenders. Remember, you are more likely to succeed in a rent to own arrangement if you use the rent to own term to show you can pay your bills on time and improve your credit score.

There you have it. Seven common reasons you can lose your chance at a mortgage. Rest assured the situations we discussed above are not insurmountable. You can accelerate your chances of qualifying for a mortgage with the right rent to own arrangement and some diligent effort on your part.

CHAPTER 4

17 Smart Reasons to Rent to Own

The emergence of rent to own home activity has largely been due to the current economic conditions in the United States. Many Americans have been affected by the current economy, whether it's by the stock market declines, job layoffs, foreclosures, or bankruptcies, many have felt the impact which has led people to change the "traditional" way they had lived their lives. Canadians have also felt the pinch. Bank regulations have been altered, making it harder for the average Canadian to qualify for a mortgage to ward off issues that occurred in the United States. Many Americans lost their homes or are on the verge of losing them because they cannot afford their monthly payments anymore (particularly if they hold adjustable rate or sub-prime mortgages). And, many people have seen their credit scores badly damaged. Which means there's little hope of getting another mortgage until they successfully improve their credit or find a way to save up a larger down payment than was accepted in the past.

Most people aspire to be homeowners because there are plenty of benefits, including profit potential, tax deductions, security, etc. If you lack the means to put a down payment on a home right now, but you want to see your rent money actually go toward buying a home, rent to own is an excellent option. Let's go over "equity" first. Equity is a key benefit of renting to own versus just renting.

#1 BUILD EQUITY IN RECORD TIME

Equity is among the numerous benefits of homeownership and rent to own. You can start to build equity the day you move it, which is much earlier than the day you go on title. In a well laid out rent to own deal, a portion of your monthly rent payments will actually go toward an investment — toward equity in a home. Every month a portion of your rent payment is credited towards your down payment. Over time this amount adds up that is credited toward the purchase price when you exercise your option to buy the house at the predetermined end of the rent to own period. During the rent to own term, your equity accumulates much faster than with a conventional mortgage you may get through a bank or lender. That's because you are not paying interest during your rent to own period. That means 100% of your option premium payments is applied towards the purchase of the house. To make this a bit more concrete, let's assume the future purchase price of the house you are renting to own is $300,000. Your initial down payment was $12,000. Each month you pay a $417 option premium on top of the rent for 36 months which adds up to $15,000 fast. At the end of three years, you would accumulate about $27,000 ($12,000+$15,000). Now you have $27,000 of equity in the home. In fact, the $27,000 is subtracted from the $300,000 purchase price at the end of the rent to own term. So you will actually be buying the home for $273,000.

#2 BUILD UP A DOWN PAYMENT IN RECORD TIME

To increase your chances of qualifying for a mortgage at the end of the rent to own term, it is best to end up with a down payment of 5 to 10 percent of the future purchase price. If your future purchase price is $281,000, the lender will expect you to have to have from $14,000 to $28,000 for the down payment, depending on your credit situation, income, debt and other factors. If you start your rent to own arrangement with a zero down payment, each month be prepared to aside around $583 to build up a $28,000 down payment over three years. That's $583 on top of the rent.

On the other hand, if you come in with an initial down payment of even 5 percent, you will accumulate your $28,000 down payment by paying a $259 option premium each month on top of the rent. No doubt, this is a much more manageable option premium than $583.

Ultimately, if you want to reduce your monthly payments and still save up a 10 percent down payment within three years, you need to kick start your down payment credit by putting some money down. Some investors and rent to own companies will accept a 3 percent down payment. Others will ask for 5 percent or 7 percent down. The more your initial down payment, the lower your monthly payments will be and the faster you will accumulate a 10 percent down payment to impress the lenders at the end of your rent to own term.

HOMEBUYER BEWARE TIP

Calculate how much of a down payment you will accumulate in your rent to own arrangement. Will that be enough? Run the total by a mortgage broker before you sign the rent to own contracts. A credible rent to own company or mortgage broker may be able to tell you whether the amount you accumulate will help you qualify for a mortgage in two, three years or four years.

If you are still not convinced whether you're better off putting any money down on your rent to own, here are some numbers to show how your monthly payments can go down as your initial down payment goes up. Remember, these numbers are based on a future purchase price of $281,000. Plus the goal is to help you accumulate a 10 percent down payment credit at the end of a four-year rent to own program.

Your Initial RTO Down Payment	Your Total Monthly Payment (Rent and Option Premium)	Down Payment Credit (Monthly Option Premium)
3% or $7,500	$2,122	$572
5% or $12,500	$1,983	$433
7% or $18,750	$1,810	$260

This example is based on a four-bedroom, two-story house in a high-demand community. The total monthly payment consists of fixed rent of $1,550, (fair market rent for the area) and an option premium that gets credited toward your down payment.

Looking at the chart above, it should be easier to see how your monthly payments go down when you have a higher initial down payment.

#3 MINIMAL OUT OF POCKET EXPENDITURES

As a homebuyer, you save on mortgage insurance and closing costs when you enter a rent to own arrangement (you take on those expenses when you exercise our option to buy the house). When you exercise your option to purchase the house, you will however, have to probably come up with thousands of dollars to cover both. It is nice to know that you have some time to save for these expenses. In some towns or municipalities, first-time buyers can save some money on closing costs. For example, first-time homebuyers in Toronto, one of Canada's major cities, are eligible for a rebate of the Toronto Land Transfer Tax. Be sure to ask your mortgage broker or your real estate lawyer about the taxes you may be liable for on the future purchase of your home. They should also be able to advise you if any rebates apply to your situation.

HOMEBUYER BEWARE TIP

Once you get approved for a mortgage at the end of the rent to own, be sure to budget for closing costs (include legal fees and disbursements). You can contact a real estate lawyer to get a better idea of the costs. For more information on closing expenses, see Chapter 13 (Closing Countdown: Exercising Your Option to Purchase).

#4 YOU DON'T NEED FIRST *AND* LAST MONTH'S RENT

When you buy through a rent to own arrangement, you may not need "last month's rent", but in your first month be prepared to pay your initial down payment, along with your first month's rent and your option premium amount. All of these payments should be pre-determined before you move in, so there should not be any surprises. Remember, each month's option premium amount and initial down payment are going to be credited back to you at the end of the rent to own term so that you can qualify for a mortgage. All of those details should be spelled out in your contract.

#5 YOU CAN CHOOSE A HOUSE YOU LOVE

Rent to own allows you to choose any house that will serve your family's needs and budget. If a seller will not agree to a rent to own arrangement, look for companies in your area that can help you rent to own the home you wish to own or they can help you find one just like it. Whether you are choosing from an "inventory home" or house hunting the traditional way, the house you love the most will match your family's needs and budget.

HOMEBUYER BEWARE TIP

Not all rent to own companies offer you the opportunity to select your own house. Some companies actually have inventory homes they are trying to sell you. Be sure you love the house you want to buy and can see your family thriving there for years to come. Your passion for the home can dramatically increase your ability to succeed with rent to own.

#6 YOU BENEFIT FROM ANY IMPROVEMENTS YOU MAKE DURING THE RENTAL PERIOD

In a rent to own agreement, you are to assume typical homeowner responsibilities. This includes repairs, maintenance and making improvements to your house. After all, the more you improve the home, the more its value can grow, which means more equity in your pocket. Once you take over ownership of the home, you may start to see a financial benefit for any added-value improvements you made during the rent to own term. Most realtors or rent to own companies can advise which improvements can give you the biggest bang for your buck.

#7 MORE TIME TO FIX YOUR CREDIT

If you have blemishes on your credit report, you will need to improve your score to qualify for a great mortgage terms. Be realistic. It takes time to elevate a score. A rent to own arrangement buys you that time. On average, a rent to own arrangement lasts three years, but can be as short as two years or as long as four years. Most families in our rent to own program are in it on average for three years. In most cases this is plenty of time to fix credit issues while building up equity in a home you will soon own.

To improve your credit faster use the Credit Repair Worksheet included in the bonus pack you receive with purchase of this book. To claim your bonus pack email: info@renting2own.ca

> *HOMEBUYER BEWARE TIP*
>
> *Credit repair is not easy. But your effort can go a long way. Be proactive about fixing your credit issues. Use your rent to own time wisely. Doing a rent to own does not mean that you will "magically" qualify for a mortgage at the end. If you do not use the next few years to mend your credit situation or improve money management habits, there is a very good chance that you will not get qualified for a mortgage at the end of the rent to own term.*

#8 MOVE IN QUICKLY

Once you find a home that you love, you can typically take possession of the home within 30-60 days. Gathering up your paperwork, finding the right home and reviewing the rent to own contracts can be the most time consuming part of the whole process.

> *HOMEBUYER BEWARE TIP*
>
> *Don't rush into a rent to own arrangement even if you have the chance to move in quickly. Take the time to meet a mortgage professional. If you do rent to own without getting advice from a mortgage broker or a reputable rent to own company, you could get more house than you may qualify for in the future. Before you start moving in, meet with a mortgage expert to make sure the future purchase price of the home you're going for is not too high for the income you have today. If your income increases in the future that is a bonus, but you should use current numbers to evaluate affordability.*

#9 YOU CASH IN ON THE BENEFITS OF WORKING WITH REAL ESTATE PROS

Location! Location! Location! Anyone who knows how to make money on residential real estate will tell you location of the house is key. But how do you know which neighbourhoods or types of houses are going be worth more in the future? When you work with a rent to own company, they will get rich advice. Their team of professionals can help advise whether the house you want to rent to own will in fact be a good investment for you in the long run. Realtors that work with rent to own companies typically understand the housing market better from an investment perspective. They can offer great insights on how to find a house that will continue to grow in value well after your name appears on the title or deed. After all, that's one of the easiest ways of making money in real estate and getting ahead.

#10 YOU CAN EARN FREE MONEY FROM INCENTIVES (SOMETIMES)

Did you know you could earn free money towards your down payment? Some rent to own companies offer such incentives. You can get a cash incentive just for paying on time or improving your credit in record time. Many smart homebuyers in our rent to own program are actually cashing in on incentives. How does it work? When the homebuyer meets a pre-determined objective, they earn a cash-based bonus. That means a top up is automatically added to the down payment credit they are building up each month. For many homebuyers that work with us, this can add up to more than $3,000 over a three-year rent to own term. What landlord offers that in a typical rental arrangement?

#11 YOU CAN PROFIT WHEN REAL ESTATE VALUE GOES UP

The price you will pay for the house at the end of the rent to own term is determined before you sign the contracts and must be specified in your Option to Purchase Agreement. If you lock in at a $280,000 purchase price in three years and the market price of this home is more than $280,000 at the end of your rent to own term, you still get to buy it for the same $280,000. If appreciation of the home's value is significant during your rent to own term, you can refinance your home after you take ownership and keep the profit from the appreciation. You can use this money to make more appreciation-oriented improvements such as finishing the basement.

HOMEBUYER BEWARE TIP

Look to do a rent to own in areas where there is potential for real estate values to rise steadily or rapidly. Any increase in the home's value during your rent to own term means extra money in your pocket. A real estate agent or a rent to own company should be able to give you more information about the appreciation rate in the neighborhood where you would like to own a home.

#12 TRY BEFORE YOU BUY

Consider it a neighbourhood test drive! Rent to own affords you the opportunity to try before you actually buy the home. Depending on the agreement, you can walk away if you find something seriously wrong with the house or the neighbourhood. Walking away is not advised, but it can sometimes be the best option. Especially in situations where the neighbours are undesirable or expensive repairs surfaced or government officials announced unfavourable re-zoning plans for that area. Although you will lose the option premium and down payment credits you accumulated, that amount may be much less than if you bought the house outright and tried to leave it later. Our recommendation is always to stick it out to the end, exercise your option to purchase and then sell. Ultimately the choice is yours.

#13 YOU HAVE MORE FLEXIBILITY AND CONTROL

You will have full control of the home and can maintain it and often, make improvements during the rent to own period. Smart improvements made to the property will almost always increase the value. That could mean additional equity in your pocket when you buy the house at the end of the rent to own.

#14 PIECE OF MIND IN ANY REAL ESTATE CLIMATE

A rent to own arrangement can offer some piece of mind whether the real estate market goes up or down. For example, if property values plummet, you can negotiate with the investor to continue renting (include the option in your contract). Should property values go up by the time your rent to own term ends, you may be exercising your option to purchase at a 'below market price' because you locked in your purchase price a few years ago. In this case you would be putting extra money in your pocket.

#15 NO RISK OF FORECLOSURE

Pretend for a minute you are a homeowner. Say house prices drop, you lose your job and the lending criteria gets tighter, making a refinance almost impossible. Such a scenario has led millions of Canadians and Americans into foreclosure and, as a result, damaged their credit. If, on the other hand, you opted to do a rent to own and chose to break the agreement, there is no foreclosure process. There is simply the opportunity for a clean break and your credit is unaffected.

HOMEBUYER BEWARE TIP

Once you sign a rent to own contract, it is legally binding. If you choose to cut the lease short, you may have legal action taken against you.

#16 YOU HAVE SOME PROTECTION FROM REAL A ESTATE CRASH

As a would-be homeowner who entered a rent to own agreement, you can escape drastic property value drops easier than if you were locked into a mortgage. If you locked in to buy the house for $280,000 at the end of your rent to own term and property values plummet, you do not have to exercise your option to purchase the home. If the market collapses and the home appraises below $280,000, you can choose to cut your losses and walk away. If you walked away from a mortgage, on the other hand, you would lose a lot more, including your credit rating.

HOMEBUYER BEWARE TIP

If you choose to walk away at the end of your rent to own term, you will lose the initial down payment including the monthly option premium money you paid over the term of the contract. This can add up to a substantial amount of money. Be sure to weigh the pros and cons of walking away.

#17 NO MORE RENT INCREASES

In a rent to own arrangement your monthly costs are fixed for the duration of the rent to own arrangement. This includes your rent and the option premium amount. Your future purchase price is locked in too. Once you sign the contract, you have piece of mind that those numbers will not change.

Overall, there are plenty of benefits to rent to own. Not all of them will apply to your current situation, but at least you know the extent of the benefits and can pick and choose which ones make sense for you. Now that you've read this chapter, you are in a better position to figure out which benefits will have the biggest impact for you. Grab a piece of paper and a pen. Quickly jot down the benefits that resonated with you. If you go down the path of negotiating your rent to own terms with a private seller or a rent to own company, refer to this list to ensure you are getting the benefits that are important to you.

Check out the Glossary at the back of this guide if you are stumped by some of the words or real estate jargon used in any of the chapters.

CHAPTER 5

8 Little Flaws of Rent to Own

In Chapter 4 we summarized the many benefits of taking the rent to own path to get into homeownership. It would be extremely erroneous to not discuss the pitfalls of rent to own. We uncovered many of these juicy details over several years. By summarizing the downside of rent to own here, we hope we save you some time and effort. The good news is that the list of cons is shorter than the list of pros. Let's review some disadvantages of rent to own:

#1 MORTGAGE RATES MAY RISE IN THE FUTURE

Both Canada and the United States have been seeing mortgage rates at their lowest since the 1950's[6]. It is hard to predict whether the cost of borrowing rates will be any lower in the next decade. If you wait too long before entering a rent to own agreement, you may be facing higher mortgage rates when it comes time to exercise your option to purchase at the end of your agreement. The sooner you start to rent to own, the sooner you can take advantage of the historical low interest rates. On the other hand, once you get into homeownership with a conventional mortgage, you may still be impacted by higher mortgage rates in the coming years when you go to refinance your mortgage (maximum term you can hold a mortgage is five years). The saving grace is that your house should appreciate in value every year, which will likely offset the borrowing costs.

#2 HIGHER MONTHLY PAYMENTS

Monthly payments will be higher than a typical rental. Bottom line. But it isn't always as a result of the rents being outrageous. In a rent to own scenario, you must account for your option premium. This amount is part of your monthly payment and it is instrumental in helping you build up a down payment to qualify you for a mortgage. The monthly option premium is paid on top of the rent and should be credited (100 percent) towards your down payment at the end of the rent to own term. The amount you accumulate through the option premium will constitute your down payment. It will be deducted from your future purchase price by the investor when you purchase the home. The downfall is that you may

---

[6] Source: www.propertywire.com, *"Property Investment in the US is Cheaper Than Ever With Mortgage Rates Lowest Since 1950s"*

have to tighten your purse strings for the next few years so that you can afford to pay the option premium each month to build up your down payment.

HOMEBUYER BEWARE TIP

Understand the total down payment credit you can accumulate by the end of your rent to own term. Be sure to get it in writing. Make sure you are prepared if the lenders want a bigger down payment than what you accumulated during your rent to own term. You may not qualify for a mortgage unless you can come up with more money on your own. If you cannot meet the lender's down payment criteria, in most cases you will have to walk away from the home and any down payment credits you may have accumulated.

#3 YOU ARE RESPONSIBLE FOR REPAIRS

You need to budget for repairs around the house. Although you are not listed on the mortgage (yet), in a rent to own agreement you are to assume typical homeowner responsibilities. This includes repairs and maintenance. Many people in our rent to own program see this as more of a 'pro' rather than a 'con'. After all, the more you maintain and improve the home, the more its value can grow. Ultimately you can enjoy the financial benefits once you get your own mortgage and become the owner of the house you've poured your heart and soul into.

HOMEBUYER BEWARE TIP

Before you enter into a rent to own agreement, insist on a home inspection. This will help uncover any major issues with a home you are about to rent to own. Don't you want to know whether the roof needs to be repaired? Whether there are mold issues? Or if the electrical system is up to code? Whether you uncover significant issues, or identify odds and ends that need fixing, you will be in a better position to decide whether to budget for repairs or walk away from a possible money pit.

#4 LATE PAYMENTS CAN VOID YOUR AGREEMENTS

If you have a history of being late on rent or bill payments and aren't willing to change stale habits, rent to own may not be the best option for you. On the other hand, if you are determined to start paying on time and in some cases reduce spending, rent to own could work wonders. Let's face it; if you want your situation to change, you need to do things differently. Rent to own makes you more accountable for your actions. You have to be totally committed to improving your situation because you will now have something to lose (your down payment and the house) if you fall back into your old habits.

#5 OWNER OF HOUSE GOES INTO FORECLOSURE

During the time that you are renting to own a house, the homeowner/investor can fail to make payments on the original mortgage on the house. In this case the bank will take ownership of the house and the homebuyer is forced to move. The rent to own agreement may be voided. Be sure to consult with a lawyer about how you can protect yourself. Although this rarely happens, it's important to be aware of it. One of the best ways to avoid this situation is to work with a reputable rent to own company that has a large pool of investors they can vouch for.

6 NO GUARANTEE YOU'LL QUALIFY FOR A MORTGAGE

There is no guarantee that a bank will give you your financing at the end of the rent to own period. You still may not be able to buy the home for the same reasons you couldn't buy at the start of the rent to own term: bad credit, insufficient down payment, not enough income. You may need to forfeit your down payment purchase or find someone to co-sign your application. Bottom line is that you must be prepared to work on repairing your credit and pay on time to accumulate your down payment. No one else can do it for you.

> *HOMEBUYER BEWARE TIP*
>
> *If you don't go ahead with your purchase, you usually have to forfeit the down payment you accumulated. To improve your chances of qualifying for a mortgage, use the rent to own term to improve your credit issues. Also, prior to signing a rent to own contract, make sure you will end up having enough down payment at the end of the term and that your income supports the future purchase price of the home. Many rent to own companies will help you with this calculation. For a second opinion, see a mortgage professional to help you estimate what mortgage you can afford. Alternatively check out the online calculators banks offer.*

#7 YOU CAN LOSE MONEY IF YOU ARE NOT THE "COMMITMENT TYPE"

The fact that rent to own is a commitment is the not the disadvantage. In this way, it is no different than carrying a mortgage. The disadvantage is if you decide not to go along with the purchase at the end of the rent to own contract. In most cases you are likely to lose the down payment you accumulated through the monthly option premium payments, plus the initial down payment you paid at the onset of the rent to own agreement. This is simply the seller's/investor's safety net for providing you flexible financing terms.

HOMEBUYER BEWARE TIP

Before you sign the contract, find out what happens if you choose not to exercise your option to buy the home. Be sure you know how much you stand to lose if you choose to walk away from the purchase at the beginning, middle and end of the rent to own term.

8 YOUR CLAIMED INCOME AND DEBT DETERMINES THE HOUSE YOU CAN AFFORD

Lenders and mortgage brokers follow specific guidelines to determine the maximum mortgage you can qualify for. Your household income, credit situation, monthly debt payments (credit cards, car lease, student loans, etc.) all impact how much you can afford. For example, if the future purchase of the house is too high for the income you state on your income tax returns, there is a very good chance you will not qualify for a mortgage at the end of the rent to own term. Even if you completely fulfill your rent to own obligations, lenders may not approve you for a mortgage if the price of the home is higher than your claimed income can support.

HOMEBUYER BEWARE TIP

Before you sign the contract, understand the maximum you can afford to spend on a house and stick to that limit. This is critical to help you budget your monthly expenses as well as plan for the future purchase price of the home. Taking the time to do this can help you succeed with your rent to own arrangement.

Securing a mortgage is tougher these days, and for those with blemished credit histories, it can be nearly impossible to get approved. If you are looking to build equity while improving your credit history, you may find rent to own a strong match for your situation. But as with anything in life, you have to weigh the pros and cons to determine whether rent to own is for you.

Families that are successful in our program see more benefits than disadvantages when it comes to using the rent to own approach to get into homeownership. The key is to have realistic expectations. In our experience, the main reason a rent to own arrangement can fail to work for tenant buyers is because they may have expected miracles. Please remember that just because you are in a rent to own does not mean that you will "magically" be qualified for a mortgage at the end of the term. In our program, "blemished credit" is the most common reason families opt to buy a home through a rent to own arrangement. Credit repair is not easy, but a little consistency, diligence and hard work goes a long way to ensure the homebuyer's success.

If you're not set on using the rent to own period to repair your credit score, improve money management habits or to build up your down payment, there's a very good chance lenders will turn down your mortgage application in the coming years. A combination of focus, effort and discipline are required to improve your chances of getting a mortgage at the end of your rent to own term. This is especially true if you are doing this in tandem with a partner or spouse. It is crucial that you are both on the same page.

CHAPTER 6

Two Ways to Rent to Own: Which is Right for You?

Now that you are more familiar with the pros and cons of a rent to own arrangement, you should know the different ways these arrangements can be structured. Essentially there are two ways of setting up a rent to own deal; either you go house hunting in search for a home that suits your budget and criteria or you choose from an inventory of homes that have been pre-selected for rent to own.

Each approach offers you advantages and disadvantages. Let's take a closer look.

Scenario A: You Found a House You'd Love to Own

In some cases, people find a house before they find out that they cannot qualify for a mortgage. In other cases, people get a fantastic opportunity to purchase a house they are already renting. In these situations, either people approach the landlord directly about renting to own their property or the landlord approaches the prospective homebuyer. In either case, the house comes first. That's the easy part. Figuring out whether it is a good fit for a rent to own arrangement can be challenging.

To help determine whether the house can be financed under a rent to own arrangement, here are some questions you need to answer;

1. Is the house located in a good area? Are homes growing in value? Is the growth potential good?
2. What is the future purchase price? Is the future purchase price negotiable?
3. What appreciation rate was used to calculate the future purchase price?
4. Does your income and down payment support the future purchase price of the house?

5. Is the seller interested in financing the rent to own arrangement? If they are looking to sell outright you'll need another investor on board.
6. What down payment do you need to accumulate to qualify for a mortgage at the end of the rent to own term?
7. How much of your monthly payment goes toward your down payment credit? Will that be enough to help you qualify for a mortgage?
8. What is the condition of the house? How much work does it need?

A seller who wants to rent to own their house privately to you is already holding the mortgage on the house. Try to find out what motivated them to rent to own the house in the first place. Are they eager to get you into the house because they may be facing financial difficulties? This could be a red flag. Financial difficulties often lead the seller to default on their mortgage. In this case the lender can foreclose on the owner after you move in and start your rent to own term. If the house goes into foreclosure unfortunately you would lose your initial down payment and any other down payment credits you accumulated. Although this is an unlikely scenario, you do need to be realistic. Financial troubles can blindside anyone and some people go to crazy extremes, even if it means doing it at your expense.

HOMEBUYER BEWARE TIP

In a private sale-rent to own deal, the seller may not be able to transfer title to you if the seller has financial problems or judgments registered against the title. On the other hand, if you use a rent to own company, they may have measures in place to protect you in this scenario. It is up to you to bring up this "what if" question.

In a private rent to own arrangement, you may not be working with a realtor. That is a significant drawback because it is harder for you to verify that person you are dealing with is the actual owner of the home. You may request a copy of their mortgage and have it reviewed by your lawyer to ensure authenticity.

HOMEBUYER BEWARE TIP

If you are thinking of trusting someone with thousands of your hard-earned money, be sure to get some assurance that you are dealing with the rightful owner of the home. Protect yourself from con artists who may be trying to pull a fast one, and don't actually own the house they claim to own.

If for some reason the landlord/seller is not interested in financing the rent to own arrangement, contact a rent to own company in your area. There may be a rent to own company that is willing to broker the rent to own arrangement on a home that you found.

Scenario B: Qualify for Rent to Own First

In this situation, a home has not been secured for the purposes of a rent to own arrangement. You actually go house hunting *after* you have qualified for a rent to own arrangement. Investors or rent to own companies typically help you find a house that meets your needs. But before you hit the streets and start shopping for a house, you get evaluated to ensure rent to own is a good fit for you. The process often involves completing some paperwork to prove your income so that a house-hunting budget can be established based on your circumstances. In many cases a realtor will be involved to try to find a home that matches your budget and wish list. We prefer to qualify the homebuyer first. Then we involve a realtor to start looking for a home and the homebuyers are actively involved in this process. All of our homebuyers work with realtors once they are approved for our rent to own program.

HOMEBUYER BEWARE TIP

The seller of a home covers realty fees. So you don't have to worry about paying the realtor for their time. But some investors or rent to own companies charge you an application fee as high as $500. Be sure to ask if there are any fees you should be aware of before you decide to work with a rent to own company.

When you go house hunting for a rent to own home with a realtor, what should you expect? For starters, the realtor can present a competitive market analysis (CMA) to give you an overview of current market trends and recent sales in the area you are interested in. They usually have a better understanding of what buyers can get for their money. An agent will also offer a wealth of information about the neighbourhood's schools, shopping, property taxes, population and future growth.

Depending on your area of choice and time of year, there may be many listings that match your criteria. Realtors typically filter and weed-out properties that are not a perfect match to your requirements, hopefully resulting in a shorter search cycle for you. There is nothing worse than looking at 100 homes, none of which meet your wish list. Once you find a house you love, the realtor will often use the CMA to negotiate a fair purchase price. Typically, the realtor will work with the investor on the actual "offer" since it is the investor who will have to secure the mortgage against offer to purchase. Although you are not buying the home today, the lower the purchase price is for the investor, the more likely they are to pass on the savings via the future purchase you will be locking into. Refrain from making assumptions. This is something you should discuss in advance with the investor.

Working with a realtor adds a layer of sophistication and legitimacy to the rent to own house hunting process. A realtor will typically help to advise you about neighbourhoods and home values. Plus they can confirm the investor you are entering into a contract with is legitimately on title of the house you are renting to own. This can be harder to prove if you are dealing with a seller privately.

Most importantly, a realtor can help complete the purchase. Once an offer has been accepted, the realtor can arrange a home inspection and ensure that all repairs and stipulations in the purchase agreement are completed. A licensed realtor can ultimately save you time and money. Ultimately they validate that you are involved in a legal real estate transaction.

Are you sure that a mortgage is not in the cards in the next few years? Do you have some time before you need to move? Getting approved for a rent to own program with a credible company allows you to investigate what a rent to own arrangement can do to help you become a homeowner before you spend time looking at houses.

Rent to Own an "Inventory" House

In this approach, an investor or rent to own company may have secured a house (or several of them). They may opt to sell it outright or find a homebuyer who wishes to rent to own. Because the home was acquired before a homebuyer was in place, we refer to it as an "inventory" house.

With this approach, the house is often advertised as rent to own and the owner will usually do showings, take applications, and filter prospective homebuyers – similar to the usual rental process. Often there may be several inventory homes available for you to choose from. This can save you a lot of time, if you need to move fast. However, if the house you desire is an attractive property, the rent to own company may have to sift through many applicants vying for the same house. Often the homebuyer with the more sizeable down payment gets approved over others. On the other hand, if you are the homebuyer who gets approved for an inventory home, the house is likely available for occupancy and you can move in sooner.

Which Type of Rent to Own is Best?

There is no right or wrong when choosing to go with an inventory home or shop for a home from scratch. Which approach you choose is often a matter of personal preference or circumstance. Do you want a house that was recently renovated to someone else's taste or do you prefer to make cosmetic upgrades to suit your needs? Do you need to move in within a few weeks or do you have some time to look around for the right house?

In some instances companies that assist with rent to own may dictate the approach. If their business model dictates that they acquire the home first and find the homebuyer second, you may have no choice but to select a home from their inventory. These companies often concentrate on specific areas or neighborhoods. They try to acquire homes below market value. In many cases they fix them up to boost the selling price that is presented to you. An inventory house is usually vacant, so you can move in quicker. When time is of the essence for some homebuyers, this can be a big plus.

HOMEBUYER BEWARE TIP

Be sure to choose a home that you LOVE – not just a house that is available. If you don't love it, you may leave it before the end of your rent to own term. Don't risk losing a lot of time and money if you cannot see yourself enjoying a home for the next five years, or longer.

It can be expensive for companies to cover expenses on an inventory house, especially if the house has been sitting vacant for awhile waiting for a homebuyer. The incurred expenses can sometimes be hidden in the price of the home that is presented to the homebuyers. This can make inventory homes a little pricier for homebuyers. If you have some time to go house hunting, you may find home prices are slightly more favourable or more negotiable. Your goal should be to get the best value out of your rent to own arrangement. Take your time and investigate a few different options. Compare the prices of the inventory homes against similar homes being sold in the neighbourhood. Sometimes you can find a house that is priced lower because it needs some cosmetic work. If you opt to rent to own a home, you can renovate or redecorate to add value to the home. Plus you'll likely save money on the future purchase price and set yourself up for equity growth.

Which approach is the best? Everyone's situation is unique, but as a rule of thumb consider these six questions:

1. Which scenario offers you a house you can see yourself enjoying for the next five years?
2. Which scenario allows you the time to conduct an inspection?
3. Which scenario allows you the time to crunch numbers?
4. Which scenario allows you to save the biggest down payment?
5. Which scenario will give you time and support to improve your credit score?
6. Which scenario will allow you to qualify for the mortgage based on the future purchase price? .

The key is to choose what you love – whether it is a property you are currently renting, found in inventory or it is listed for sale on the open market. In our program, once the homebuyers are qualified, they eagerly start house hunting. Sometimes it takes as many as 10 or 15 showings to find "the one". Many of the families we work with find this process exciting and exhausting – but well worth the effort. At the end of the process they are content and satisfied that they left no stone unturned (with the help of a patient realtor) in finding a place they can see themselves enjoying for years to come.

CHAPTER 7

How to Recognize a Rent to Own Scam and Protect Your Money

Scams have become a bit more sophisticated than in the past, but they are still easy to spot if you know what to look for. So what does a rent to own scam look like? In some cases, the proponent of the scam will find a nice home that is listed for sale, rent, or rent to own on the internet. They will copy the pictures of this property and mimic the available information. To complete the information loop, they will do a quick public records search for the homeowners' information so they will not be stumped if there are specific questions asked about the property. Unfortunately though, most people that end up being scammed do not ask any questions, which is what gets them into trouble in the first place.

One of the first places people start to look for rent to own opportunities is on Craigslist and Kijiji. The ads often jump out and grab your attention, like this one below. The dead give away that it may be a scam, in many cases comes after you decide to respond to the ad.

```
Stating a discriminatory preference in a housing post is illegal - please flag discriminatory posts as prohibited
Avoid scams and fraud by dealing locally! Beware any arrangement involving Western Union, Moneygram, wire transfer, or a landlord/owner who is out of the country or cannot meet you in person. More info

Rent to Own Home in Denver - 1200 sq ft 3 bdrm

Date: 20   06-07, 12:54PM CDT
Reply to: see below

Rent to own this 1200 sq ft 3 bdrm home. $199 covers your first months rent and security deposit. Each month after will be $650 a month. Contact for more information.

please flag with care: [?]
    miscategorized
    prohibited
    spam/overpost
    best of craigslist
```

This ad, even though generic, provides clues about how genuine it is. This particular one is very vague about the house, the neighbourhood and who is posting this ad and why. The main hook here is the lower monthly payments.[7]

---

[7] The online ad example is courtesy of Craigslist.

Although it may be hard to see from this example, the gist of this ad is that you can get into a rent to own by paying $199, which will cover your security deposit and your first month's rent. What you don't know, or at least would not know until you contacted the poster is that the "company" offering the rent to own is located in New York, not Denver. Does this make sense to you? Who will you be meeting and how will the transaction be completed if you were to move forward?

Spidey senses tingling yet?

Some more due diligence will start to unravel the scam. In this case, you would write back to the "company" saying that you would like to come see the property before you agree to anything. They reply with the full address of the property but insist on you mailing a cheque for $199 before they provide additional details on the property or move forward with the rent to own process. That is a dead giveaway that this may be a scam.

HOMEBUYER BEWARE TIP

There are scammers out there who are trying to rent to own homes that aren't theirs. If an online ad offers something that sounds "too good to be true", it often is a ploy to scam people out of their money.

Rent to own scams can be subtle threats, especially because they often target people who are frustrated with their current situation and are desperate to move fast.

If you're tired of renting, can't qualify for a mortgage and are short on credit or down payment money a rent to own may sound inviting. You may be inclined to act immediately, especially if the house is move-in ready. Before you reach for that phone, consider how you are protecting yourself from a scam like this true story:

Michelle Smith, self-employed and her husband Andrew Bryan lost their life savings when they learned they were being evicted from the home they were renting to own in Scarborough, Ontario, Canada. "We had put money down," said Smith. "We gave them everything we had," she told a Toronto Star newspaper reporter. Smith explained that they received eviction papers in the mail from the real owners of the house and had to move out three months later.

The company that brokered this rent to own arrangement never owned the home this family was renting to own. An investigation revealed that this company was operating for two years, pretending to be the owner of a house they wanted to rent to own to families. This company preyed on people like Smith and Bryan, who could come up with an initial deposit but in reality could not afford the home.

Smith and Bryan said they lost more than $50,000 in this situation. "We went to the police and what they said to us is this may be a civil matter," said Smith. It was later discovered that three other people in the Greater Toronto Area fell victim to a similar scam.[8]

In our experience, about 20 percent of people who pursue a rent to own arrangement never research the company representative or seller they end up working with, this is especially true if people need to move into the house in a hurry. Reputable companies have websites. They answer the phone, return calls and are happy to meet you. Their website can be an excellent source of information about rent to own as well background information on the company. But do not stop there. Call to ask questions. Meet them in person. You can even go as far as asking for references from other homebuyers they have helped. In some cases the homebuyers may be open to being contacted to discuss their experience with a rent to own company.

Knowledge and awareness are the two most effective ways to safeguard yourself and avoid becoming a victim of a scam or a faulty rent to own deal. Although there are never any guarantees, you can virtually eliminate the possibility of being scammed. Before you start responding to the ads you find online, give anyone money or sign any contracts, make sure you are not getting scammed like this couple from Midland, Texas. It is a perfect example of why you need to take this chapter seriously.

Midland police arrested Jerry "Smith" and Clare "Smith" for allegedly defrauding a couple on Craigslist in a rent to own scheme. Investigators allege Jerry and Clare knowingly sold their property that was in foreclosure by their creditors to another Midland couple without disclosing the financial solvency of the property.

In May 2011, the victims saw a Craigslist advertisement for a rent to own a home. The couple responded to the ad and set up a face-to-face meeting. The "Smiths" allegedly told the victims to write them a $6,000 check for the down payment and said they would be responsible for a monthly payment of $550 for nine years. All four people signed the contract. Without doing any due diligence (legal review of the documents), the victims handed over their money and moved in without as much as a home inspection. The victims proceeded to pay the "Smiths" three monthly installments of $550 (on top of the $6,000) before the bank moved in and sent them notice to vacate as the house had already been foreclosed on.

---

[8] Source: www.thestar.com, "Lease-to-own Housing Plan Leaves Renters Cold"

After unsuccessfully trying to reach the "Smiths", the victims were forced to file a police report and subsequently the "Smiths" were arrested. Unfortunately at this point, the victims have still not received their money back and have since had to relocate to another property.[9]

The Warning Signs

If you know what to look for, it is usually easier to recognize a scam. Here is a list of some warning signs to keep an eye out for.

MONTHLY PAYMENT PRICE IS LOW

The price listed in the ad is much lower than what other houses in the area are going for.

THE OWNER IS 'AWAY' OR ABSENT

Often the owner of the house is travelling somewhere and cannot meet you in person.

NEED MONEY BEFORE SHOWING THE PROPERTY OR SIGNING CONTRACTS

Some fake ads lure you in with "too good to be true" pricing, pictures or descriptions. They sometimes ask you to send payment if you want to see the property or find out more information. In many cases the "seller" even asks for money before contracts are in place. Do not agree to pay any money before you sign any contracts that specify exactly what you are entitled to.

CORRESPONDENCE IS IMPERSONAL

Typically the responses to your enquiries are generic templates and do not reference anything specific you may have included in your correspondence. In many cases the correspondence is also written poorly or in broken English.

PRESSURE TACTICS ARE USED

In their correspondence they may urge you to act fast or else you will miss out on the house or the low price. This is a deliberate tactic to pressure you into handing money over to them faster.

---

[9] Source: www.mywesttexas.com, *"Property Crimes Occur During Housing Crisis"*, by James Cannon.

MONEY MUST BE WIRED SOMEWHERE

Scammers often rely on this tactic. It is harder to trace money if it is wired or transferred to a bank account that is in a different country. A genuine seller will deal with local banks in your area and will encourage a paper trail rather than ask for cash.

How To Protect Yourself

The first step is to understand *who* the scammers are targeting. Scams often target people who are desperate to save money or move in fast. In reality, it is hard to find a rent to own house that will have the same monthly payments as a one-bedroom basement apartment. So when an ad promises the house is move-in ready and has a very low monthly payment, with blind faith people want to be the first to scoop it up. To motivate a reader to act, scammers will often include photos. Of course the photos are not legitimate. Scammers pull photos from real "for sale" or "for rent" ads, and post as their own. The low price and attractive photos give the scammers an upper hand. People fear the house may go fast, so they act quickly. In the rush of it all, they do not get all the details or ask questions before they hand over their money.

So how can you protect yourself from falling victim to a scam? The answer is simple – plan and do your due diligence! Planning starts with knowing what it is you're trying to achieve. If you don't know where you want to end up, how will you know when you get there? Once you've planned what you want to achieve, make sure your partner, spouse or family members are on board. Two heads are better than one when it comes to making home purchase decisions. Due diligence starts with you doing some research. First check if any rent to own properties are available in your area. A realtor or mortgage broker can help point you in the right direction. Continue by preparing a list of questions. In Chapter 11 (*18 Rules of Success*) we provide a comprehensive list of questions you should be asking. Be sure to understand the answers from whomever you are considering doing the rent to own deal with. Remember, information should be free. Getting answers to your questions should be free as well. No one asked more questions about rent to own than Andrea, a single mother from Brampton, Ontario, Canada.

Andrea was looking to get back on her feet after a very tough divorce. Feeling swindled and defeated by her ex-husband, Andrea needed a fresh start for her and her two young kids. She knew that she was not going back to renting after having enjoyed homeownership during her eight years of married life. With an income of $71,000, she could comfortably afford a house in the $250,000-$260,000 range. But she had only $8,000 as a down payment and her credit was low.

Rent to Own Essential Guide for Homebuyers

Having heard of some scams, Andrea was looking for assurance that she was not setting herself up for failure if she ended up in rent to own arrangement. Building up her down payment and improving her credit were her priorities and she was looking for a rent to own company to support both. We were one of the companies Andrea met with. She came armed with two pages worth of questions and was not shy about putting us in the hot seat:

- *When and how is my future purchase price calculated?*
- *If an appraisal is needed, who pays for that?*
- *What happens if the appraisal shows the house is worth less than the future purchase?*
- *What portion of the rental payment will be credited toward my home purchase?*
- *Who is responsible for the property taxes and maintenance?*
- *How do I build equity in the property?*
- *Is it possible to get a refund for a portion of my payments if I can't get a mortgage?*
- *Would one late payment cause the contract to be voided?*

We did our best to address each and every concern that Andrea had. Three days later, she confirmed her intent to apply for our rent to own program. Three years flew by for Andrea. In January 2014, she will be taking over the ownership of the house and can truly celebrate her fresh start.

No matter how informed you may feel about rent to own after reading this guide, be sure to research the companies you are considering working with. Ask plenty of questions. Despite all of the benefits of rent to own, success partially hinges on your level of comfort with the person/people you are entering into an agreement with. Asking plenty of questions is one of the rules of success we cover in Chapter 11 (see rule #13). The comprehensive list of questions we cover there can get you started.

HOMEBUYER BEWARE TIP

If you are doing a rent to own directly with a seller, be sure to have the title on the property checked. This is to make sure that the correct owner of the home is giving you the option to purchase. Your lawyer can help you with a "title" search. Do not skip this step. This is the good way to make sure your rent to own arrangement is legitimate.

An ounce of planning truly leads to a pound of value when it comes to your security and financial well-being. Take the time to scrutinize the person/company that is offering the rent to own. Do your research. Ask questions. Understand the contracts you are signing. These simple actions will make it harder for anyone to scam you or take advantage of your situation and put you in the line of potential failure.

CHAPTER 8

Will *You* Qualify for Rent to Own?

More and more people are looking at rent to own as a way to stop renting and start owning, but not everyone can qualify. Just like banks can turn people down for a home loan, some people may not be a good fit for a rent to own arrangement.

In the past, Americans and Canadians typically executed a rent to own arrangement on an individual basis, with loose qualification criteria and a handshake. There really wasn't a formalized process in place to evaluate whether the homebuyers could succeed with a rent to own. Many rent to own deals continue to go through privately in this manner. We often hear how these deals are executed; the qualification process tends to be loosely structured and the terms of private arrangements tend to be more in favour of the landlord-seller. Homebuyers are lured by low monthly payments but in the long run failed because they did not save up a big enough down payment. So when their mortgage application fell through, so did their hope of homeownership.

But today, as a prospective homebuyer, you have more choices. There are many reputable companies that are completely dedicated to the residential rent to own industry. Perhaps we can go as far as saying these companies have helped make rent to own arrangements more professional and mainstream. In some cases, other companies share our philosophy --- making rent to own a win-win arrangement. We work hard to ensure fairness and transparency for the homebuyers – even when they fail to ask all the right questions.

Qualification Criteria

You can start by speaking with a rent to own company. Across Canada and the United States there are a number of rent to own companies that have designed their business models to help people achieve the dream of owning their own home, when they cannot qualify for a home loan. These companies often have a "qualification" process, similar to a bank or mortgage broker. If you are interested in working with a rent to own company, you can expect they will evaluate your income, debt situation, credit history and the amount you can put down today.

When applying for our rent to own program, many people are surprised that there is a down payment requirement. In fact, the two most popular questions we get from our applicants are; *"why do I need a down payment"* and *"how much of a down payment do I need"*?

It is a good question – there are several reasons. Remember, we do not carry an inventory homes. We allow the homebuyers to shop the open market. When they find a house, we match them with an investor who can buy it and wait for 36 months to sell it back to them. Just like a bank requires you to have some "skin in the game" to off-set their risk in underwriting your mortgage, the investor is looking to minimize their risk in case you will not hold up your end of arrangement to buy the house for a set price at a set date. Your initial down payment acts a little like an insurance policy or a safety net for the investor. Think about it from the investor's point of view. Say the house you want to own is $250,000. For the investor to secure that house for you, they need to qualify for a mortgage. That means the investor has to lend their good credit rating to your cause, plus they need to come up with a 20 percent down payment (which is what most lenders want if the property is not the investor's primary residence). Based on those lending terms, the investor has to come up with $50,000 cash to get the mortgage. But that is not all. The investor will most likely also have to spend money on a lawyer, closing fees and land transfer tax. Let's see how these add up for a $250,000 house purchase:

Investor's Cash Outlay on our Rent to Own	Amount
20 percent down payment	$50,000
Lawyer/closing fees (may be less or more in your area)	$1,600
Land transfer tax (may be less or more in your area)	$2,500
Total	**$54,100**

In the example above, the investor has to come up with about $54,000 in order to secure a home that you can rent to own within a few years. It is easy to see that the investor is making a big financial commitment to help you get into the house you want. So it is reasonable for the homebuyers to expect to have a down payment to show they are committed to their goal of homeownership. Homebuyers in our program would have to come up with a down payment of $7,000-10,000 to rent to own a $250,000 house.

Are there rent to own programs out there that do not require a down payment? Probably. But if you want to successfully reach your goal of owning the home, we would definitely advise against "zero down" arrangements. The reason is simple. Your initial down payment forms an important foundation to help you accumulate the money needed to qualify for your own mortgage. Think of it this way, the down payment gets you that much closer to homeownership plus it quickly adds up to your equity in the property. In a "zero down" rent to own deal, be prepared to save thousands of dollars on your own to get qualified for a mortgage.

HOMEBUYER BEWARE TIP

Any rent to own arrangement where you accumulate 5 percent (or less) of the future purchase price, puts you at a higher risk of not being able to qualify for a mortgage, especially if the mortgage rules get any tighter in the coming years.

Sarah and Tony from Orillia, Canada were tired of renting. They wanted to start their married life together in a new home. Sarah responded to a private ad for rent to own in their local newspaper. When they visited the house, they loved what they saw. The house was less than 3 years old in a new development. The owner indicated the future purchase price of the house would be $255,000. He enthusiastically encouraged them to move in right away. The seller was comfortable with a monthly payment of $3,000 – and no down payment was required. Plus the seller was willing to count $400 each month towards their down payment on this house when they decide to purchase it outright. Sarah and Tony were eager to jump on the opportunity! Luckily, a smart uncle helped them do the math. With only $400 a month going towards their down payment, at the end of the three-year term, Sarah and Tony would save about $14,400 – roughly 4 percent. Not bad.

Just then Uncle Sam threw out the "what if" question. "What if the bank rules change and you need to come up with a 7-10 percent down payment to get the mortgage in your name?" That means, on their 255,000 purchase, a lender could ask for a $17,850 - $25,500 down payment. With little certainty about how mortgage criteria may unfold over the next few years and whether $400 a month was going to get them a mortgage, uncle Sam urged the couple to reconsider this rent to own opportunity.

Ideally the seller should have modified the rent to own terms a little bit to include an initial down payment. That would help the couple kick start their down payment savings. This alone would have helped Sarah and Tony accumulate a down payment credit of more than $24,000 - a substantial enough amount to offset tighter mortgage rules of the future. Here's a quick look at the numbers.

Important Numbers to Consider	Zero down	Money down
Future purchase price (after 3 years)	255,000	255,000
Goal: 10 percent down payment (at the end of 3 years)	25,500	25,500
Your initial down payment	0	10,000
Monthly Option Premium ($400 on top of rent over 3 years)	14,400	14,400
Total down payment accumulated	14,400	24,400
Amount you may need to save to get a mortgage (10% down)	11,100	1,100

Let's be honest, saving can be difficult in the best of times. Most people who opt to save on their own tend to get sidetracked. With an inadequate down payment, there is a high probability the lenders will turn you down for a mortgage. In the event you cannot secure a mortgage, you will forfeit all of the money you paid to the landlord-investor to date. Plus you will be asked to leave the property. In the end, you were really nothing more than a renter all along.

HOMEBUYER BEWARE TIP

If you do not have a reliable plan for building up a down payment while you are in a rent to own, you are better off renting.

The main factors that should come into play when you are being 'qualified' for a rent to own;

- Your annual stated income
- The amount of your down payment
- Your credit report
- Your debt load

If you have recently come out of a consumer proposal or bankruptcy, you may need a few extra years in a rent to own program to rebuild your credit. Rent to own is especially useful for people looking for a positive fresh start.

HOMEBUYER BEWARE TIP

If you are in the middle of a consumer proposal or bankruptcy be sure to give yourself at least two years to repair credit before applying for a mortgage. Be sure to discuss your situation with a mortgage broker before entering a rent to own arrangement.

CHAPTER 9

The Key to Saving Money When You Rent to Own

Don't even consider signing a rent to own agreement before you do a home inspection. Insist on one. This is the key to potentially save you thousands of dollars in the long run. You wouldn't buy a used car without having a mechanic look under the hood, would you? Most likely you wouldn't even buy a used car before having it safety inspected. Inspecting the physical condition of a house is an important part of the home-buying process (and rent to own process) and should not be overlooked, even if you have to move into the home in a hurry. A professional home inspector will look for defects or malfunctions in the house's structure, such as the roof, plumbing, or foundation. An inspection can uncover pest infestations, dry rot and similar damage that can cost a lot of money to repair.

A properly trained, certified or licensed home inspector will analyze your house as a system, looking at how one component of the house might affect how another component works or how long it will last. Home inspectors will go through the house and perform a complete visual inspection to assess its condition and all of its systems. They will identify the components that are not performing properly as well as point out items that are beyond their useful life or may be unsafe. An inspector will also identify areas where repairs may be needed or where there may have been problems in the past. Inspections are intended to help you as the homebuyer better understand the condition of the house, as observed at the time of the inspection.

The home inspector will do a visual inspection by looking at the home's various systems, including interior and exterior components. The inspector will check exterior components including roofing, flashing, chimneys, gutters, downspouts, wall surfaces, windows, doors, the foundation and the grading around it.

The interior systems that the home inspector will check include electrical, heating, air conditioning, ventilation, plumbing, insulation, flooring, ceiling and walls, windows and doors. The inspection of the interior systems is visual, meaning that the inspector will not make openings to inspect behind walls or under the floor.

If your home has character and features a wood-burning fireplace, for example, your inspection should be bit more customized. In Canada, home inspectors must be WETT (Wood Energy Technology Transfer) certified to inspect a wood-burning appliance, such as a fireplace or wood stove. Many home inspectors will not carry out a WETT inspection as part of the standard home inspection unless it is requested. A WETT inspection will add at least one hour to the inspection time. If you have a house with a chimney, be sure the seller has it cleaned first so that it can be properly inspected. This can be arranged in advance with the house seller.

If your inspection takes place in the winter, you may need to adjust your expectations, especially after snowfall or on a cold, icy day. The roof and the foundation may not be fully visible for inspection if they are covered with snow and ice. For safety and insurance reasons, the home inspector would not typically climb up on the roof in those conditions. However, typically the home inspector will inspect the roof from the ground or other vantage point. This also applies to the chimney and downspouts. In the winter months it may also be challenging to test the air conditioning unit. In cold climates, you can damage the compressor if you try to run in when the temperatures are below 65 degrees. Some sellers may agree to have an amount held in escrow until you can have the air conditioning unit tested in the spring. This is something your realtor and lawyer can help negotiate.

Whether your inspection takes place in the summer of winter months, always ensure it takes place in daylight and is done by a professional inspector. It is not a good idea to conduct an inspection at night, with a friend, since a number of the very important components of the house may not be inspected properly, or missed all together. Helen found out first hand how an inspection saved her potentially thousands of dollars.

Helen had been looking for a house for three weeks when she came upon what seemed to be the perfect fit for her. It was a tidy, cozy three bedroom semi-detached house in Brampton, Ontario, Canada. It hit 90 percent of her needs and wants. Helen visited the property a second time after work one evening with the realtor and invited along her contractor friend to give her a second opinion. For Helen it was comforting to have a friend's expert point of view. Helen's contractor friend scrutinized over the visible parts of the house and in the end gave her the thumbs up. She was excited, everything seemed to be falling into place and she was on her way to a fresh start after an ugly divorce. As part of the rent to own arrangement, we also had a licensed inspector walk through the house. New to the process, Helen questioned why a home inspection was even needed. We explained that the inspection is a mandatory step to protect the homebuyer and the investor.

The inspection revealed a layer of dark green mold, about an inch thick in the attic of the house. It turns out that the previous owners replaced the tiles on the roof so that the house looked great from the outside but never bothered to clean up the boards on the inside of the house, hoping to cover the mold up, rather than cleaning it up. The purchase of the house was put on hold and eventually cancelled, since the expense to clean up and repair the problems in the attic was prohibitive. Unfortunately for Helen, the mold the inspection uncovered was a deal-breaker. Helen was extremely disappointed but it was short lived. She fell in love with another house that was just listed. It was two streets away and it passed the inspection.

"My first instinct was to avoid the professional inspection on the first house. That house looked perfectly clean and well kept. I didn't even think about the attic," Helen admitted. "But honestly, the home inspection saved me thousands of dollars, not to mention the health concerns and headaches of having mold removed.

As a homebuyer, your rent to own contract will probably state that fixes and repairs are your responsibility from the moment you move in. You need to know what repairs the house needs so you can decide if you can afford to take on those projects. Without an inspection, Helen would have been stuck with a house full of mold that would potentially cost her thousands to remove. Dealing with the unexpected expense of mold removal, Helen may have missed monthly payments on the house and could have been facing eviction. In reality, she averted the risk of losing the house along with her initial deposit of $10,000.

What's Included in a Home Inspection?

The home inspector generally provides a written report that documents the condition of every major system and component of the home. The report is usually available same day or within 24 hours of the inspection. If problems beyond the scope of the inspection are found, the home inspector may recommend further evaluation.

Typically, a home inspection does not include appraisals or quotes for repairs and does not determine compliance with regulatory requirements. A home inspection is not intended to provide warranties or guarantees about the condition of the house or how well it works.

Many home inspectors' associations have a code of ethics that prevents home inspectors from offering services to repair or improve homes they have inspected. While they may provide you with a personal opinion on the repairs and a range of costs involved based on past experience, it is recommended that you obtain three independent quotes from qualified contractors for the repair of any defects or deficiencies identified during the inspection.

So how much does a home inspection cost? A standard inspection is usually $300-500. If the house has unique features like a wood burning fireplace or septic tank, the cost may be higher. Who covers the inspection costs? Typically the homebuyer, since they are the ones that need to determine whether they still want the house after they see the inspection report.

> *HOMEBUYER BEWARE TIP*
>
> *Be sure to choose a house that will likely pass the home inspection. In most cases, you will have to cover the costs for each failed inspection. That means you may fall several hundreds of dollars short on your initial down payment.*

It is often said that one of the most expensive and important purchases you will ever make will be your home. However, unlike the guarantee a buyer receives with most purchases, there's no money-back guarantee or return policy if you're not satisfied with your rent to own home. Once you move in, you're on your own to anticipate problems, maintain it, repair it, and pay the bills. An inspection will help you anticipate potential problems before you move in and prevent you from getting in over your head and over your budget.

CHAPTER 10

The ABC's of Rent to Own Agreements

A typical rent to own arrangement should involve two separate agreements. These agreements are legally binding documents that should detail the arrangement. They agreements essentially outline roles and responsibilities, timelines and pricing. They are designed to protect you and the landlord-investor should someone not hold up their end of the agreement. You should expect to sign at least two contracts; Option to Purchase agreement and Lease (Rental) agreement. If the agreements you are presented with are not two separate documents, be sure to ask the landlord-investor to separate the Lease agreement from the Option to Purchase agreement.

HOMEBUYER BEWARE TIP

To protect yourself, always get two separate agreements rather than one 'all-inclusive' contract. Although it is not common practice, some unscrupulous sellers have been known to find a reason in the Lease (Rental) agreement to cancel the whole transaction. Having two separate agreements in place provides homebuyers with more protection.

Once you sign the agreements, they govern what the landlord-investor and you, the homebuyer can and cannot do during the rent to own term. These agreements are legally binding contracts and can come into play if ever you or the landlord-investor take legal action against each other. If your partner is also signing the agreements, the landlord-investor can enforce the agreements against both of you should the need arise. It is crucial for everyone involved to understand what their responsibilities are under the terms of the Option to Purchase agreement as well as the Lease agreement.

How the Agreements Protect You

No question, agreements can be nerve-wracking if you do not know what to expect. Having some insights into what these agreements contain may help reduce some of your anxiety. That is why we put together the list below. It summarizes at a very high-level what information should be captured in the two agreements so that your interests are protected;

- The legal names of the landlord-investor and homebuyers
- The legal address of the house you are renting-to-own
- The monthly payment you agreed to pay (without utilities)
- The date when the monthly payment is due (for example, the first day of the month)
- The amount and terms of any initial down payment, the monthly option premium, incentives
- Will you be responsible for repairs? If so, do repairs need to be completed by a certain date?
- Who is responsible for maintenance?
- The length of the rent to own agreement.
- The conditions under which your option premium (or incentives) can be withheld
- The conditions under which you can be evicted
- The conditions for satisfying the rent to own agreement and purchasing the property
- The rules or restrictions for subletting
- The rules and restrictions about cosmetic and structural changes to property
- Details on how and when the landlord-investor (or their representative) can enter the property
- The procedure for making changes to the agreement

HOMEBUYER BEWARE TIP

Unless you are moving in with your own appliances, you will want to ensure that fridge, stove, dishwasher, washer and dryer are all included in the rental agreement and that they are also included with the purchase of the house at the end of the rent to own program.

In an effort to protect all parties involved in our rent to own arrangements, we have invested thousands of dollars to perfect the agreements that are signed by homebuyers and investors. If you are doing a rent to own deal privately you should have some legally binding agreements in place between you and the landlord-investor. Be sure to at the chart we provided detailing what the Lease/Rental agreement and the Option to Purchase agreements should contain.

Rent to Own Essential Guide for Homebuyers

Option to Purchase Agreement	Lease or Rental Agreement
Length of rent to own term (eg. date ownership will transfer)	Length of the rental term
Future purchase price	Monthly rent, what's included
Initial deposit amount (down payment)	Number of occupants
Amount going towards your down payment each month (option premium)	Which utilities you are responsible for
Total down payment amount that you can accumulate if you pay on time	Maintenance and repairs obligations
What happens if you default on rent	Penalties for late or non-payment
What happens if you default on the option premium	Consequences for non-payment (eg. eviction)
What happens if you default on your option premium	Responsibilities of landlord-investor
What happens if you choose to walk away at the end of the term	Responsibilities of homebuyer
Assignment rights	When/how property manager/landlord can enter the premises
Responsibilities of landlord-investor	Sublet or assignment restrictions
Responsibilities of homebuyer	Rules about pets (if any)
Reasons the agreement may be terminated	Rules about extended absences
Under what conditions the home will sell to the homebuyer	Reasons the agreement may be terminated

Please remember the information in the charts or this chapter does not constitute legal advice. We urge you to seek legal advice from a real estate lawyer in your area, ideally a lawyer familiar with rent to own.

Although the info captured in the chart is extensive, we encourage you to speak to a lawyer, preferably one who may be familiar with rent to own. A good lawyer will help to ensure your agreements suit your specific situation.

When you are at the stage of reviewing draft agreements, you or your lawyer may uncover something in the agreements that you do not agree with. Perhaps there is a phrase or two that needs to be altered. Be open about discussing it with the landlord-investor prior to signing the agreement. It is completely acceptable to have multiple rounds of revisions of the agreements as you and the landlord-investor try to reach a compromise that all sides are comfortable with before anything is signed.

The Most Important Agreement

The Option to Purchase agreement is essentially the agreement that will dictate the terms of the purchase of the house. Because each homebuyer's situation is unique, no two agreements are the same, but there are similarities. For example, most Option to Purchase agreements do state that homebuyers who are renting to own a house are often responsible for the maintenance and repairs of the house. By the way, to some this might seem unfair at first. However, it also gives you as the homebuyer more control and flexibility to make the house your own or make improvements that matter to you in the long run.

The Option to Purchase agreement also includes the term – depending how long you will be renting to own. In our program, that can be anywhere from one to five years. Together the investor-landlord and the buyer-tenant agree on a future purchase price. This price is written into the agreement. The future purchase price is fixed and will not change. Each month, the homebuyer pays an extra amount on top of the monthly rent that is outlined in the Lease agreement. This extra amount is often called the option premium. Many people refer to this as forced savings. The option premium turns into your down payment money. The nice thing is that this sum of money can add up fast. Imagine having more than $12,000 at the end of a three-year rental period (based on a $350 monthly option premium). The agreement should state exactly what amount you can accumulate and how it will be applied towards the down payment when you exercise your option to purchase the house. Often the landlord-investor is allowed to use the option premium money however they see fit, as long as they credit the full amount to the homebuyer at the end of the term. Essentially this involves the seller (investor) to take the accumulated down payment off of the pre-determined purchase price.

At the end of the rent to own term, the homebuyer has the option to purchase the house for the pre-determined price indicated in the agreement. If as a homebuyers you are unable to qualify for a mortgage for any reason, you are at risk of losing the house along with all the money you put in or accumulated through the monthly payments. Your contract should explicitly outline what happens if you cannot get a mortgage or choose to walk away at the end of the term. On the other hand, if you are able to qualify for a mortgage, there may be additional conditions that the investor wants you to meet in order for the sale to go through. This may include meeting a specific timeline or additional charges may apply. Be familiar with any other conditions that must be met in order for the purchase to go through.

HOMEBUYER BEWARE TIP

No matter how eager you are to hand over your money or move into a house to kick off your rent to own arrangement, you must allow yourself enough time to have your agreements sorted out and reviewed by a lawyer. In most cases it will take at least two business days. Be sure to guide the appointment with the lawyer in advance and advise the landlord-investor or rent to own company that you will seek legal counsel before you move in or make any payments.

Purchase Ahead of Schedule

What if you can qualify for your mortgage ahead of schedule? Say you win the lottery or come into some money. You may qualify for a mortgage earlier than expected. Some investors may be happy to let you purchase the house earlier so they can free up their money. Ideally this is something you negotiate into the Option to Purchase agreement before you sign.

Keep in mind the investor probably locked into a mortgage for the original length of your rent to own. Lenders usually charge a hefty penalty for breaking a mortgage early. Typically that penalty is paid by the homebuyer if they choose to purchase ahead of schedule. A penalty to break a mortgage can sometimes be anywhere from one thousand to five thousand dollars, depending how much time is left on the mortgage and who the lender is. If you choose to exercise the option to purchase earlier than the date indicated on your agreements, the investor or rent to own company should be able to confirm the penalty amount after speaking with their lender. Be sure to factor in mortgage penalty costs (if any) if you think that you will be able to land a mortgage approval earlier than the terms outlined in your agreements.

What You Need to Know About the Lease Agreement

The Lease agreement simply states what you will pay monthly for rent and for a specific period of time. This agreement specifies obligations and responsibilities of the landlord (investor) and you, the homebuyer. It includes what the landlord and homebuyer have agreed upon in regards to rent payments and length of the lease agreement with respect to the rent to own arrangement. It also explains what the house came with, what upkeep is required, how renovations should be handled and what the rules are about subletting or extended absences. Terms of eviction should also be outlined here. Should the homebuyer stop paying rent, a landlord-investor has the right to evict, provided they follow the legal protocol to do so. If a grace period is applicable, it should be listed in this agreement. Just like with the Option to Purchase agreement, the Lease agreement can be altered before you sign, if you find something in there that you may not agree with, provided you're dealing with a reasonable investor.

HOMEBUYER BEWARE TIP

If you are doing a rent to own directly from the owner of the house, have a real estate lawyer review the title. First, it allows you to authenticate the person you are giving money to and signing contracts with is the legitimate owner of the house. Second, you can confirm there are no impairments or liens that will prevent you from purchasing the home. This proactive measure is especially relevant when you are entering a rent to own agreement directly with a landlord-investor.

Get Legal Advice Before Paying Rent to Own Dues

Yes, rent to own can be an amazing opportunity for potential homeowners, but you must safeguard yourself. Rent to own arrangements can be complex. You should treat rent to own the same way you would treat any house purchase. We always encourage our homebuyers to consult with a real estate lawyer before signing any contracts or paying any fees to the rent to own company or landlord-investor. A lawyer can help you understand the full scope of your rent to own commitment and its financial implications. Caution should not be thrown to the wind under any circumstances.

HOMEBUYER BEWARE TIP

Your lawyer may suggest having some clauses in the agreements re-worded. Whether you are doing a private deal directly with the seller or landlord-investor or working with a rent to own company, they should be willing to consider the amendments you are suggesting. Moreover, they should be open to modifying the agreements. If the investor or rent to own company is reluctant to amend the agreements without providing you with a satisfactory explanation, consider whether you will be comfortable working with these people for several years. It is never too late to talk to someone else about a rent to own arrangement.

Rent to Own Essential Guide for Homebuyers

After reading this chapter you should be more familiar with the two different agreements that typically apply to a rent to own arrangement – that is a great start! Plus you should have a better understanding of roughly what each agreement covers – this should help to make you more comfortable about negotiating favourable terms that protect your interests before you hand over money or move in.

Ultimately, agreements are intended to protect everyone's interests in a rent to own arrangement. Sure, they can be intimidating because legal terminology is difficult to understand and a rent to own deal can be complex if you are not familiar with the process. Fortunately, there is nothing complicated about making an appointment with a lawyer. Even if you have to borrow the money to pay for the lawyer's fees, it is money well spent. In fact, it should be the only money you spend before you sign anything on the dotted line.

> *HOMEBUYER BEWARE TIP*
>
> *A rent to own company should provide all of the agreements for you to take to your lawyer. Always try to find a real estate lawyer that is familiar with rent to own so that you get objective advice. If a lawyer is unfamiliar with the rent to own concept, they may be uncomfortable addressing your questions or concerns.*

CHAPTER 11

The 18 Rules of Success

Rent to own is a great option for people that have decided that it is time to start building equity in their own property instead of paying for someone else's property as a renter. But you have to be realistic about what rent to own can and cannot do for you. The people who are likely to succeed in meeting their goal of becoming a homeowner are prepared to follow some specific rules. In this chapter we are summarizing the rules to help you succeed in a rent to own arrangement. We can say from experience, homebuyers who are most successful in the rent to own program we established take these rules seriously.

RULE #1: SET YOUR GOALS

It is not enough to say: "I want to rent to own a home". You need to create your "big picture" goal. What do you want to get out of a rent to own arrangement? The answer should always be the same; homeownership.

Remember, a rent to own arrangement does not guarantee you will get a mortgage. During your rent to own period, you must hit smaller targets (discussed in Chapter 3) to achieve your goal of homeownership. The clearer your big picture goals, the easier it will be for you to stay on course and qualify for a mortgage.

RULE #2: SCRUTINIZE RENT TO OWN ADS

Although there are many legitimate posters on Craigslist, Kijiji and other online sites that post rent to own ads, you should be wary. Warning bells should go off if you are asked to pay application fees or to send money to in order to get more details or see the house.

RULE #3: FIND THE "RIGHT" HOUSE, NOT A HOUSE THAT IS AVAILABLE "RIGHT NOW"

So you are browsing through the online classifieds and an ad grabs your eye: *"Rent to own this beautifully renovated 3 bedroom house with no money down. No credit."* Sounds great! You make an appointment to see it. Good news – it is clean, has nice features and you can move in ASAP. Sounds like it meets your immediate needs. But is it going to fulfill your needs in the future? Do not be motivated by the "move in quick" benefit. Falling for a house that is available "right now" rather than a house that is "right" is a common reason homebuyers fail in a rent to own program. One homebuyer who took on an inventory house told us they were either disappointed with the neighbourhood or the size or the layout. Realizing that they don't want to buy this house in the future, they choose to break their rent to own agreement and cut their losses. They chose to walk away from more than $10,000. If they continued to rent for an extra month while they waited for "right" home to come on the market, they may have saved themselves thousands of dollars.

You must love, love, love the home you choose to rent to own. We cannot stress this enough. We always work with our homebuyers to find the right house for their budget and their needs. And it pays off. Homebuyers see more than one house and have the ability to compare them. This helps uncover what they like and don't like in a house. Other things we encourage our homebuyers to do before committing to a property is evaluate what they like and don't like about the area. We suggest touring the neighbourhood. Get a feel for the schools, parks, amenities and proximity to transit. One last thing we recommend is to visit the neighborhood in the evening and during the weekend. Every area looks great during the day when most neighbors are working. Are you comfortable with the vibe the neighbourhood has in the evening or on a Sunday when everyone is home? Be sure the house and the neighbourhood fill your short and long-term needs by day and by night.

RULE #4: DO YOUR RESEARCH BEFORE YOU COMMIT

If you think you know all there is to know about rent to own because you looked at rent to own ads, think again. Browsing on Craigslist or Kijiji for rent to own opportunities does not constitute research. Get to know the person(s) on the other end of the rent to own opportunity. You are entering into a serious commitment. Make sure you get to know the folks you are working with. If it is a rent to own company, ask:

- How long have they been in business?
- What makes them a strong choice for a rent to own arrangement?
- How do they help you succeed in a rent to own?
- How are they different from other rent to own companies?
- Can you speak to any of the people that have gone through their program?

RULE #5: SHOP FOR A HOUSE YOU CAN AFFORD

Some homebuyers are often surprised that the monthly rent, option premium payments and utilities are not the only costs when you rent to own. As the seasons change, expect to spend money on maintenance and repairs. Whether it is lawn maintenance or leaky faucets, keep some money aside for planned and unplanned repairs. After you put aside money for home maintenance, your monthly income should leave you enough to cover other expenses such as groceries, utilities, entertainment, car, insurance, gas or vacations. Plus you'll need a little extra to make credit card payments or perhaps pay down any other debts you carry. Take some time to establish a comfortable budget before you begin looking at houses and *stick to it*. A house that is out of your budget can result in late payments or missed payments. Late or missed payments can get you evicted. A good rent to own company or a mortgage broker should be able to suggest the optimal price range for your house, based on your present situation.

To help you plan what you can afford to spend on a house, check out the Budget Worksheet included in the bonus gift pack you receive with purchase of this book.
To claim your free gift pack email: info@renting2own.ca

RULE #6: WORK WITH A LICENSED REALTOR

If you go "house hunting" for your rent to own home, one of the easiest ways to protect yourself is to ensure that the company you decide to work with uses licensed real estate professionals to purchase the house. We never complete a rent to own transaction without a realtor. Why? They offer you some protection from fraud that a private seller cannot. Make sure you verify that a transfer of title took place when the landlord-investor purchased the house. This gives you assurance that the landlord-investor you are signing agreements with is indeed the legal owner of the house and has no liens that could stop you from taking title on the property.

RULE #7: ALIGN FUTURE PURCHASE PRICE WITH YOUR STATED INCOME

The house you're buying should be in line not only with the income you earn, but also the income the taxman has on file for you. Make sure you know exactly what income you need to claim on your tax returns to support the future purchase price of the home. Be careful not to fall in love with a house that is out of your budget (based on your stated income). Sure, you can pick up extra hours or take on extra jobs to find additional money for rent, maintenance and the eventual down payment. In reality, you may be setting yourself up for failure. Lenders use specific formulas to determine whether you will qualify for a mortgage.

Your stated income is very important in this calculation. How long you have had the job and the probability of you keeping it comes into question as well – remember Brynn in chapter 3? Besides, spending too much on a house could leave you with little money for other goals in life, such as retirement, college funds and vacations. Before beginning your house hunt, you must first determine what you can afford based on your current stated income. If you choose to work with a rent to own company, in a perfect world, they should help determine what you can afford. You can also go online and check out the house affordability calculators that most banks offer on their website. Alternatively, get some professional advice. A mortgage agent will be able to offer you a wealth of information based on your specific situation and current lending criteria.

RULE #8: TREAT A RENT TO OWN AS IF YOU ARE BUYING YOUR OWN HOME

It always amazes us how many people will put down a $10,000 down payment and sign a three-year contract after only a 20-minute glimpse at a house. The truth is, these homebuyers typically do not succeed with rent to own. Why not? They do not treat a rent to own house as if they are buying the home with their own mortgage. Remember rule #1? Is your goal to become a homeowner? With that in mind, treat this transaction as if you are the purchaser. What does this mean, exactly?

First, find a home you absolutely love! Can you see yourself enjoying it for at least five years? Second, take the time to inspect the home before you sign any agreements. Hire a professional home inspector. If you choose to save money and bring in friends or family members to inspect the home, are you confident they know what to look for? Take extra precautions not to buy into a money pit, especially if the house is more than 15 years old. Repair costs can end up costing you the house if your monthly income falls short.

RULE #9: AVOID "ZERO DOWN" ARRANGEMENTS

If you are serious about getting into homeownership via rent to own but are living pay cheque to pay cheque, start saving your down payment (initial deposit). You will improve your ability to succeed with rent to own if you come into the arrangement with a down payment. To get into a rent to own program, expect to come up with at least five percent of the selling price of the house you are interested in. Some rent to own companies or private sellers may accept less, but be prepared to pay a higher monthly option premium in order to accumulate a sufficient down payment to qualify for your mortgage at the end of the rent to own term.

We cannot help but stress the importance of having an initial down payment. Here's an example of how quickly your down payment adds up to 10 percent over three years if you come in with a down payment of either 3 percent, 5 percent or 7 percent on a house that is currently selling for $250,000 and has a future purchase price of $281,000.

Rent to Own Essential Guide for Homebuyers

Your Initial RTO Down Payment	Your Total Monthly Payment (Rent and Option Premium)	Down Payment Credit (Monthly Option Premium)
3% or $7,500	$2,122	$572
5% or $12,500	$1,983	$433
7% or $18,750	$1,810	$260

This example shows that just by paying $260 on top of your rent, you can accumulate more than a $28,000 down payment credit over three years if you come into the rent to own with a 7 percent down payment. In addition to the monthly option premium payments, the homebuyer would also pay fair market rent of about $1,550. This example is based on the investor purchasing the house today for $250,000 and setting a future purchase price of $281,000.

In a rent to own, you typically do not need first and last month's rent – just a down payment along with your first monthly payment when you get the keys. Why not kick start your rent to own down payment savings with the money you would have used for last month's rent?

HOMEBUYER BEWARE TIP

Be sure you will be in a position to afford the mortgage you will apply for at the end of the rent to own period. That means staying within your budget when choosing a house even if it means you can't get as much house or as polished a house as you want right now. Consider rent to own as a stepping-stone that will take you closer to the home of your dreams.

Keep in mind that every rent to own company or independent seller will have their own requirements for when the down payment is due. For example, we do not collect any money from our homebuyers until the home inspection is completed. Be sure to ask when the down payment money is required, so that you can ensure that everything is in place on your end and things move along smoothly.

RULE #10: APPRECIATE HOW YOUR FUTURE PURCHASE PRICE IS SET

Ask what appreciation rate will be used to calculate your future purchase price. If you ask no other questions but this one, you will be miles ahead of other homebuyers who jumped into a rent to own arrangement with blind faith. Many private investors and rent to own companies may apply a standard, across the board appreciation rate that can be as high as six or seven percent per year. Watch out! This may inflate the price you pay for your house in the future. In reality, many areas will have lower annual appreciation rates than seven percent. For example, properties in the downtown core often appreciate at a higher rate than homes north of the city. On the other hand, homes in urban areas appreciate faster than in rural areas. There are ways to determine what the fair appreciation rate should be. A professional realtor can assist, if you're looking for an objective opinion. They can help evaluate how homes are selling in the area. They can also illuminate trends and development plans that may add value to an area. To get more details you can contact the planning and development government offices in the area where you are house hunting. Once you have a better idea of the fair appreciation rate for the area where you would like to own, ask the investor what annual appreciation rate is being used to determine the future purchase price of the house. You should make sure you are not overpaying for the house at the end of your rent to own term before you commit to anything.

RULE #11: WORK TOWARDS A TEN PERCENT DOWN PAYMENT

You should be suspicious of anyone who promises that you can own a home at the end of a rent to own arrangement by making low monthly payments. In reality, rent to own usually requires a bigger monthly commitment than renting – unless you have a large initial down payment. With $15,000-$25,000 towards your initial down payment, your rent to own monthly payments may be lower. Most people come into a rent to own with about $10,000. In either case, we recommend working towards at 10 percent down payment accumulation through the rent to own program. Generally, the lower your initial down payment, the higher your monthly option premium will be in order to get you to the 10 percent goal. Having 10 percent down can greatly increase your chances of qualifying for a mortgage, especially if mortgage rules get tighter.

RULE #12: VALIDATE THE INTEGRITY THE PEOPLE YOU PLAN TO WORK WITH

Meet with each of the companies that you are considering. Face to face meetings may seem old-school, with how 'plugged in' our society is. But they are still the best way to get a feel for a company and the integrity of the people behind it. After all, you are entrusting them with your money and the roof over your head. The least they can do is meet you in person to discuss how their program works and address all of your questions.

Before the meeting, be sure to prepare a list of questions (see rule# 13). As a prospective homebuyer, you deserve full disclosure, so make sure you get it. One of things that we always offer our homebuyers is the chance to speak with one of our current homebuyers. It gives them the chance to find about another family's experience with rent to own; how things are going for them now, etc. There may be nothing more valuable than speaking to someone who has gone through the journey you're about to embark on.

RULE #13: ASK TOUGH QUESTIONS AND UNDERSTAND THE ANSWERS

Just like homeownership, rent to own is a big commitment. Make sure you know how rent to own works and what it will give you in the end. Arm yourself with questions. Be sure you get straight answers that you understand. If you are comfortable with the information provided, you will likely feel more

Rent to Own Essential Guide for Homebuyers

comfortable about moving forward in the process. But what should you ask? Most people do not know where to begin. To get you started, we provided a list of questions.

- Can I pick any house? Anywhere? Any price?
- What are the parameters for selecting a house in your program?
- How much income do I need to get the house we want?
- How long will I need to rent to own?
- How do I qualify for a rent to own?
- How much down payment is required?
- When do I pay the down payment?
- Are there any extra fees that I will have to pay?
- How much will my monthly payments be?
- How do you calculate the monthly payments?
- How much of my monthly payment goes towards my down payment or purchase price?
- How much of a down payment will I accumulate at the end of the rent to own term?
- Is my down payment refundable if I choose not to buy the house?
- Why are the monthly payments higher than if I were to rent?
- How do you calculate appreciation on the house?
- Who is responsible for repairs and maintenance on the property?
- What would cause me to get evicted from the property?
- Can I have pets?
- Can I do any renovations I choose (eg. replace carpet with hardwood)?
- Will I have to sign two separate agreements (Lease and Option to Purchase)?
- Can I review the agreements before we have to pay you?

By no means is this list exhaustive. Just like every family has unique goals and circumstances, every rent to own arrangement will be slightly different as well. We encourage you to add questions that reflect your personal circumstances and concerns. For example, if you are thinking about using a rent to own company and your credit is severely bruised, ask if credit repair support is provided and how it works.

To organize your questions and answers for quick reference, check out the Rent to Own Preparation Worksheet included in the bonus gift pack you receive with purchase of this book. To claim your free gift pack email: info@renting2own.ca

Rent to Own Essential Guide for Homebuyers

RULE #14: GET SOME SUPPORT TO IMPROVE YOUR CREDIT

One of the reasons you may be considering a rent to own in the first place is because you might have less than perfect credit. We understand. Bad things happen to good people. A rent to own can give you as much as three to five years to improve your credit score. Although this seems obvious, we have to remind homebuyers that they need to be proactive. They always seem surprised to hear that if they do nothing to improve their credit during the rent to own period, they can sabotage their chances of qualifying for a mortgage. If you rent to own through a company, find out how they might assist with credit repair.

In our experience it is best to stay away from companies that will not commit to supporting you in your credit improvement quest. Why? Well, if you had trouble improving your credit in the past by yourself, why do you think you can tackle it on your own now? More than ever, you need support because there is much more on the line – a house and the money you are putting down on that house. There is more to lose than just 'last month's rent'. To get your credit on track, all you may need is a little guidance and to be accountable. On the other hand, if your situation is more complicated, you may be steered toward a more expensive solution -- credit counseling. No matter what, be realistic. You will likely need to understand your credit report better, change your spending habits or adjust money management methods to see improvement in your credit situation. Is that something you can do solo or will you get further ahead with help? Like most people, you likely benefit from a little support to reach your credit goals. We even wrote a handbook called *"7 Truths About Your Credit"* to help our homebuyers improve their credit situation. Understanding how credit works is an important first step in the repair process. We are so passionate about helping you take this first step that we gave it away for free with the purchase of the guide you are reading now. All you have to do is use this free tool and it will make your DIY credit repair process a lot smoother.

Make a plan and take action to repair your credit. The *"7 Truths About Your Credit"* book will help you along the way. It is included in the bonus gift pack you receive with purchase of this Guide. To claim your free gift pack email: info@renting2own.ca

Be realistic. A third party won't be able to help you repair your credit if you have not taken some basic steps on your own.

- You can't raise your score if you are still disputing balances with service providers.

- You can't raise your score if your finances are still in free fall. If you're unable to pay your bills, you certainly can't fix your credit. Real credit score repair will have to wait until your financial crisis has been solved and you have enough money to cover your expenses, plus some extra to begin paying down your debts.

- You can't raise your score if you don't use credit. Credit scores try to predict how well you're likely to use credit in the future by how well you've used it in the past. So while living a cash-only lifestyle may do wonders for your wallet, it won't boost your score — in fact, without consistent use of some credit, eventually credit bureaus won't even generate credit scores.

- You don't have to pay credit card interest to achieve a great score. Know that "using credit" is not the same as carrying a balance on your credit cards. Carrying a balance is expensive, bad for your finances and completely unnecessary. Many who have achieved 800-plus scores pay off our balances religiously, and we know you can build and keep great credit scores without ever paying a dime of credit card interest.

Don't expect overnight results. You're likely to see improvement in your scores within 30 days if you pay down significant chunks of your credit card debt. But otherwise, credit repair takes time, and how much time depends on many factors detailed in your credit report, which we explain in the DIY credit repair handbook *"7 Truths About Your Credit"*. If you have serious black marks such as bankruptcy, consumer proposal or foreclosure, the credit repair checklist at the back of this guide to help you stay on track and improve your credit situation to meet the lender's requirements.

To help you set priorities and stay on track to raise your credit score, check out the Credit Repair Checklist included in the bonus gift pack you receive with purchase of this book. To claim your free gift pack email: info@renting2own.ca

RULE #15: DO YOUR DUE DILIGENCE

Unfortunately, there will always be people putting together rent to own deals who can be greedy and try to cash in on your naivety or desperation to move in quickly. Because not every rent to own arrangement is set up to lead you down a successful path to homeownership, you should spend a few weeks doing your 'due diligence'. Give yourself time to ask questions, review agreements, ask more questions, meet with at least one mortgage professional and seek legal advice from a real estate lawyer before you hand over any money.

RULE #16: INSIST ON TWO SEPARATE CONTRACTS AND UNDERSTAND WHAT YOU SIGN

If you decide to rent to own your next home, hire a lawyer to review the contracts. Don't just sign the agreements and hope for the best. This is one of the reasons that people find themselves in hot water. It's not always what *is* in the contract that makes the difference. Sometimes what *isn't* in the contract that can cause problems. There should be two agreements for your lawyer to review; the Lease (Rental) agreement and Option to Purchase agreement. Having separate agreements will discourage a landlord-investor/seller from attempting to gain your option fee by taking advantage of a lease misunderstanding.

RULE #17: USE YOUR TIME WISELY

Ultimately, a well-planned rent to own arrangement buys you time. Time to establish or repair your creditworthiness. Time to save or add to your down payment. Time to discover any flaws in the home that you will purchase. Time to get a feel for the neighborhood prior to committing to a long-term mortgage. Use the time wisely, especially when it comes to building up your credit and your down payment. How much time and effort you dedicate here can truly mean the difference between becoming a homeowner and prolonging your renter lifestyle.

RULE # 18: DO NOT RELY ON "BLIND FAITH"

Blind faith is belief without true understanding. Just because someone is letting you rent to own their house doesn't mean you will end up on title at the end of the rent to own period. Sure, an investor wants to help you. That's why they are tying up a significant amount of cash and leveraging their good credit rating so that you can rent to own the house from them. But don't kid yourself. In most cases these folks are not losing any sleep if you are not working on improving your credit score or not accumulating a sufficient down payment credit while you're in the rent to own program. It is up to you to understand what you need to do to qualify for the mortgage and work towards it during your time in the rent to own arrangement.

Your goal of homeownership can be a reality before you know it. These rules can help get you there. Some are more important than others, but in general, they all part of the roadmap to success. If you embark on the rent to own path, be sure to re-read this chapter.

CHAPTER 12

Mortgage Basics: What it Takes to Qualify

Unless you have hundreds or thousands of dollars to buy a home outright at the end of your rent to own arrangement, you will need to qualify for a mortgage to purchase the house. Understanding the main factors that lenders take into consideration can actually bring you one step closer to getting a mortgage. Lenders often look at four main factors when they review your financial circumstances to determine whether a mortgage is within your reach. These four factors include stable income, a good credit history, the property you are purchasing, and how much of a down payment you have. Together, these four factors influence whether you qualify and the interest rate you will receive.

HOMEBUYER BEWARE TIP

Before you look into a rent to own option, find out if you can qualify for a mortgage the traditional way. If the interest rate seems high or the down payment requirements are inflated, compare it against rent to own approach to determine which scenario is optimal.

Let's take a closer look at each of the four lending criteria:

STABLE ANNUAL INCOME

Your income is key when determining how much of a mortgage you can afford. In addition to calculating your annual household income, lenders consider any income changes that may impact your ability to make your payments. For example, if you and your partner are currently contributing to the household income, would you still be able to afford your mortgage if one of you lost the income or separated? That is something a lender will likely look at. What if a baby comes into the picture and your partner decides to become a stay-at-home parent? Remember Al and Monique's situation in chapter 1?

To determine whether you have stable income, lenders will want to know whether you work for yourself or whether a company employs you. If the latter, you will be qualified based on verified income. That means a lender will want to see an employment letter and pay stubs. Plus they may ask for your Notice of Assessment, which is issued by a government agency like Internal Revenue Services in the US or Canada Revenue Agency when you file your taxes each year.

On the other hand, if you are self-employed, lenders rely on what's called your stated income, rather than verified income. Stated income represents the amount you claim on your tax returns. In this case, lenders often want to see two years of financial statements and recent Notice of Assessments.

CREDIT HISTORY: INCREASE SCORE AND ERASE BLEMISHES

Mortgage lenders always review your credit report. Your credit report shows a history of how well you pay bills or repay debt. Although your most recent credit report is of interest, lenders may look at your credit history going back five or six years. Your credit report contains critical information including the credit score. The credit bureaus use a sophisticated formula to calculate your credit score. Your score is based on how you make your car lease payments, pay credit card bills, cell phone bills, as well as how much credit you are using and the type of credit it is (eg. credit cards or lines of credit). Most lenders look for a credit score of 680 or higher. Maintaining a good credit rating by making payments on time is critical to getting a mortgage. If you have outstanding loans or credit card debts, try to change your habits and start paying on time. Most importantly, settle disputes quickly with creditors to avoid going into collections. It will make a difference.

CAPACITY TO REPAY: REDUCE YOUR DEBT LOAD

When determining your budget, another important factor lenders take into account is the amount of debt you currently have. They figure, the lower your debt-to-income ratio, the more money you'll likely have to put towards your monthly payments. In addition, lenders will use your debt level to help determine what a manageable mortgage amount will be for you. This is a very important qualification criterion. Try to settle as many debts as possible before you apply for a mortgage.

CASH TO CLOSE: DO YOU HAVE THE INCOME, DOWN PAYMENT AND CLOSING COSTS

Lenders are interested in knowing your assets and your income. In fact, one of the most important questions a lender will ask is how much money you earn annually. Keep in mind they are looking for a stable paycheck. Do not think about changing jobs or careers for a few years if you plan to apply for a mortgage. Ideally, you should continue to work at the same place or job for the whole rent to own term.

It used to be that you could buy a house with zero down, but those days are behind us. Tighter lending rules means a buyer needs a minimum of 5 percent down. If you have blemishes on your credit report, you will likely need 10 to 15 percent down. Usually anything less than 20 percent down requires you to take out mortgage insurance. That means you can expect additional fees. If you have a down payment of 20 percent or more to put down, you will likely be applying for something known as a "conventional" mortgage. Lenders prefer conventional mortgage clients and waive the need for default insurance or other related premiums. A conventional mortgage means you are likelier to qualify for a loan at lower lending rate. A higher down payment also means your monthly payments may be lower, which is a great incentive.

When you get approved for a mortgage, be sure you also account for the closing costs. Be proactive because in many cases, this is something many rent to own arrangements may overlook. These fees usually include things like property taxes, title insurance, mortgage registration, and lawyer fees. When property title is transferred to your name, you will have to pay these expenses. Sometimes these costs add up to thousands of dollars, depending on the area where your house is located. These expenses should not be overlooked. Lenders will want proof that you can afford closing costs.

COLLATERAL: MAKE A SMART PROPERTY CHOICE

The house you choose to buy may influence your ability to get a loan. After all, your house is the lender's security or as they call it, collateral. If for some reason you default on your loan payments and are unable to repay the loan, the lender will become the owner of your house. Typically lenders will put the house on the market in hopes of selling it quickly and so they can recoup the money you owe to them. For example, if the house you want to buy is in an undesirable area, it may be more challenging to qualify for a mortgage because it may be harder to sell in a pinch – making it more high risk. You can expect a lender to request a property appraisal to assess the condition and market value of the property to be mortgaged. This is the lenders' way of ensuring you to have some skin in the game, especially if you are applying for a larger mortgage or still have some blemishes on your credit history. The lenders feel they are taking some risk by giving you a mortgage, so they want you to risk something too – the house. Every lender defines collateral requirements differently. That is why it is best to speak to different mortgage professionals or banks about your mortgage needs.

In a nutshell, what do lenders look for?

Applying for a mortgage can be an aggravating process. If you are prepared, you may elevate some of the frustration and disappointment. That is why it is important to be aware of the lending criteria before you lock into a rent to own arrangement. Remember, the four things lenders typically look at when you apply for mortgage include:

1. Your *Credit* history (score and history are key)
2. Your *Capacity* (to take on more debt)
3. Your *Cash to Close* (income, down payment, closing costs)
4. Your *Collateral* (lender's assurance you will re-pay your loan)

No matter how uninteresting this may seem, do take the time to wrap your head around these "4 C's". Understanding them will help you determine where you need to spend your time and effort during your rent to own term.

When it comes time to applying for a mortgage, keep these "4 C's" in mind. This is what most lenders will look at when qualifying you for a mortgage. Make sure you have these "4 C's" sorted out well before you apply for the mortgage.

What Kind of House Can You Afford?

Now you know what lenders look for when considering if they will give you a mortgage, you may still be wondering how much house can you afford? Well, that depends on the monthly mortgage payment for which you qualify. Lenders apply payment-to-income ratios that you can also use for a ballpark estimate. Your monthly mortgage payment shouldn't exceed between 28-32 percent of your monthly gross income (before taxes and other deductions). This includes principal and interest on your mortgage payments, taxes, homeowners insurance, and heating bills. Lenders will also want to make sure that your entire monthly debt, including credit card and car payments, does not exceed 40 percent of your gross monthly income, as this will start pushing towards the "house poor" side of the scale. A word of caution – lenders don't factor in the cost of maintaining a home. To play it safe, take one percent of the home's current value, divide that number by 12 and you will have an idea of what to budget for monthly upkeep. For example, if your house costs $250,000, the monthly maintenance will average out to about $200 a month. If the house is less than five years old, maintenance expenses may be a bit lower.

What Interest Rate Will You Pay?

Another question you probably have is about the interest rate you can expect. A high credit score and high down payment usually mean that you are a lower risk for the lenders. In turn, they will offer you a better interest rate. On the other hand, your mortgage rate will be higher if you have a lower credit score and modest down payment.

Even if you can qualify with tarnished credit, you will need to weigh the pros and cons of buying versus the rent to own route. Some things to consider include: is it going to be more cost-effective to have a high interest mortgage if your credit score is not high enough? Do you want to put a bigger down payment on the house than you originally planned? Are you prepared to settle for a house that is below your expectations because that is all you can afford? Consider all your options carefully.

It is a good idea to speak with a mortgage broker before you commit to rent to own. After all, you may pre-qualify for a mortgage. Understand the difference between being "pre-qualified" and "pre-approved". Mistakenly, many people use the terminology interchangeably. Being "pre-qualified" means you get a rough idea of how much you can afford to spend on a home. For example, will you be able to afford the future purchase price? The mortgage specialist will typically give you and answer based on the numbers you provide them. So if your numbers are exaggerated or incorrect, your "pre-qualification" verdict may be inaccurate. Be sure to provide accurate numbers, especially if you are trying to confirm whether you can get a mortgage today or whether a rent to own arrangement will help you qualify for a mortgage in a few years.

> **HOMEBUYER BEWARE TIP**
>
> *A mortgage "pre-approval" is much more useful than a "pre-qualification" if you are only a few months away from applying for a mortgage. In this case the mortgage specialist may dissect your credit report, examine bank accounts and debt, verify employment or analyze your credit card bills. If you are granted a "pre-approval" it means a lender has committed to giving you a mortgage, provided the house meets the lender's requirements. Also the lender is committed to holding your interest rate for a few months to safeguard you in case interest rates start to creep upwards.*

Stressful and lengthy is how many people will describe the mortgage approval process. If you understand the basic criteria lenders use to qualify you for a mortgage you can stay in control. At the same time choose the right seller or company to work with to rent to own your home. , you will not only simplify the mortgage application process for yourself, you will be in a great position to actually meet the lenders' criteria and qualify for a mortgage at the end of your rent to own term.

CHAPTER 13

Closing Countdown: Exercising Your Option to Purchase

When you enter a rent to own agreement, the purchase date seems to be far off in the future. But most of us agree that in reality time flies. Before you know it, it's time to start working on exercising your option to purchase the house so that you can become the official owner of the house. The closing date is listed on your Option to Purchase agreement – mark it on your calendar. About six months prior to this date is when things start moving forward faster than you may expect. Below we provide a summary of tasks you need to account for as you start counting down the days to your closing date, the day you become the official owner of the house your rented to own.

SIX MONTHS BEFORE CLOSING

Pull together all of your rent to own agreements. Keep them handy. Confirm with the investor/seller the down payment amount you have accumulated to date. Try to estimate how much more your down payment will grow in the next six months. You will need to know how much your total down payment will be. Also be sure to confirm when the investor (seller) will provide a letter stating your down payment amount is being credited towards the purchase listed in the Option to Purchase agreement. In many cases the letter will need to be notarized. This letter is crucial in order for you to move forward with your mortgage application.

Once you sort out the details with the investor/seller and know the down payment amount, contact a mortgage specialist at your bank or an independent mortgage broker. Let them know about your plans to apply for a mortgage. They will likely need to know things like your address, purchase price of the home (see Option to Purchase agreement), your income and down payment credit. Ask them to also help you calculate the closing costs for your house.

A mortgage broker will likely pull your credit report as well. With six months left on your rent to own arrangement, you should have time to fix any small credit problems that may still be tainting your credit report. For instance, if you have an account in collections or arrears, pay it off or get the account back in good standing as soon as possible to ensure you can meet the lender's qualification criteria (discussed in Chapter 12).

FOUR MONTHS BEFORE CLOSING

Find out from your mortgage specialist or broker what documentation they will need to get you pre-approved for a mortgage. Start gathering the needed documentation to prove your income. If you are employed, you will likely need to get a letter from work confirming your employment along with recent pay stubs and a tax bill or Notice of Assessment. Make several photocopies of each document, especially if you are planning to shop around for a mortgage. Lenders will also ask what debts you have. Plus they will want to know how much of a down payment you have and where it is coming from. They will look into your credit report, and last but not least, they will want to know about the house you are purchasing.

THREE MONTHS BEFORE CLOSING

Shop around for your mortgage. Submit the documentation you gathered up for mortgage brokers or mortgage specialists. They will use this information to verify your income and mortgage eligibility. Dig up your Option to Purchase agreement. You may need to refer to it. Ask for a pre-approval. A pre-approval is a letter confirming the maximum mortgage amount you can borrow and what interest rate would apply. If you are shopping around for the best mortgage, a pre-approval helps formalize what each lender is offering you. Mortgage pre-approvals are typically valid for 90 days. You should know that you are not obligated to follow through with every pre-approval. Shop around until you get the best mortgage rate.

TWO MONTHS BEFORE CLOSING

Set aside some money to hire a lawyer and pay for closing costs to complete the house purchase. For example, closing costs can equal 1.5 percent of the purchase price. If you are buying a house that costs $250,000, that means you would need $3,750 to complete the purchase. Closing costs include lawyer fees, and where applicable – sales tax and land transfer tax. We recommend hiring a real estate lawyer, especially one that may be familiar with rent to own arrangements. Your mortgage broker may be able to refer you.

Ask the lawyer to confirm what your closing costs will be, inclusive of legal fees. Be sure to set aside money to cover the closing costs if you have not previously budgeted for it. Provide a copy of your Option to Purchase agreement for the lawyer to review. It will help clarify the terms of the purchase and obligations on your part and the investor's part.

Decide which lender you will go with for your mortgage. Let them know you would like to proceed with a formal approval. Once you are officially approved, the lender should provide a mortgage commitment letter. The letter is your guarantee the lender will finance your purchase, provided all of the information you provided is accurate during the time your application was processed.

ONE MONTH BEFORE CLOSING

The mortgage broker may order an appraisal and a termite inspection (depending on the type and age of the home). The appraisal might be necessary to ensure that the proposed sale price does not exceed market value. If the price exceeds market value, the lender might require a higher down payment from you. That's why rule #10 (see Chapter 11) is so critical to your success if you rent to own.

YOUR BIG DAY - CLOSING DAY

On closing day you take legal possession of the house. In most cases, you will need to go to your lawyer's office to sign paperwork. Here's what you can expect on closing day:

- Your lender will give the mortgage money to your lawyer
- The investor/seller provides a letter to your lawyer confirming the amount of down payment that is being credited towards the purchase price
- You provide payment to the lawyer for closing costs
- Your lawyer will issue payment to the investor/seller
- Your lawyer transfer title to your name and registers the home in your name
- Your lawyer hands over the deed to the property to you

You made it! You finally own the home. Congratulations.
Commend yourself on completing a rent to own successfully.

Lessons Learned in Hindsight

Over four years we have counseled over 500 people just like, who want to become homeowners through the rent to own system. Although every family, every homebuyer is unique, it is easy to look back and reflect why we turned down so many people for our rent to own program. Majority of the people we have met through the years were not quite ready to embrace all of the obligations that come with rent to own. Many were not even ready to accept sincere advice that was intended to help them protect their money.

In hindsight, we can say the folks who were successful with rent to own were realistic about what it will take to succeed. They didn't blame anyone but themselves for the situation they were in. They didn't feel entitled. Quite simply, they were prepared to commit to taking matters into their own hands.

Don't romanticize the idea that some landlord-investor or rent to own company will help you succeed. These people may have genuine desire to help you — that is why they are putting some serious cash on the line. Ultimately, it is up to you to do the rest. You have to be prepared to do most of the heavy lifting. The heavy lifting starts with due diligence before you actually lock in to the arrangement. We are sharing this information because we want you to be fully informed about what it takes to succeed with a rent to own arrangement. We believe that when you are aware of the obstacles in advance, you are likelier to thrive and end up on title rather than broke, and out on the street. Plus you are less vulnerable to fall prey to unscrupulous or faulty rent to own arrangements where you could face a lot of disappointment.

If you are considering a rent to own arrangement and you are reading this, you have already taken the first step to safeguard yourself from disappointment and headaches later. You deserve to be congratulated on seeking advice about rent to own. Taking the time to educate yourself will not only help you reach your goal of homeownership, it will also help you protect your money on the way there.

CHAPTER 14

Crossing the Finish Line: Maria's Inspirational Story

We often get asked if people can actually qualify for a mortgage after going the rent to own route. Well, if the answer was "no", we wouldn't be writing this guide. Yes, indeed people do make it to the finish line and qualify for a mortgage at the end of the rent to own term. As long as you have a goal, are informed and are willing to work hard, homeownership can be your reality at the end of the course. Maria's story is a great example of that.

After Maria's first marriage, her credit score and finances took a hard hit, so she resolved herself to a life of a renter; moving when a landlord would decide to sell, leaving behind everything she put into the rental, including a kitchen she paid to upgrade. Now on her third rental, Maria, her second husband Daniel and their three young kids settled for a townhouse that didn't have enough storage space and an unfenced backyard. They were there for about three years when Maria's dad was diagnosed with a fatal illness. As she sat at his bedside, Maria learned that her dad was worried about Maria wasting her money paying the landlord's mortgage and not saving enough for the future. When Maria got home she quickly did the math and realized she had spent almost $51,840 on rent in the last three years. This was a turning point for her.

That evening Maria persuaded Daniel to look at buying a house. They both had been carrying debt from their previous marriages and their credit rating was low. They knew a traditional mortgage was not in the cards for the time being, so they called us to see if they could qualify for our rent to own program. Maria and Daniel met all but one of the criteria – the initial down payment of $6,500[10] was lacking. Discouraged, Maria felt she exhausted all options and fell back into being a renter.

---

[10] In 2010 Clover Properties had a minimum down payment requirement of $6,500. The minimum down payment requirement has increased over the years to offset increasing property values and tighter mortgage lending criteria.

Rent to Own Essential Guide for Homebuyers

When Maria's dad passed away several months later, she remembered how much it worried him that Maria did not own her own home. Her dad left behind a little bit of money for his three daughters and seven grandkids. It was a modest amount, but enough to inspire Maria to reset her goal of homeownership. Optimistically, Maria opened a new bank account and deposited her very modest inheritance. Her plan was to keep adding to it until she had $6,500 for a rent to own down payment. It took her almost 10 months from the date she opened the account, but she finally had enough money saved.

In September 2011, Maria qualified for our rent to own program and found a house that her and Daniel could call "home" – in three years time. To have a shot at getting a mortgage for their house, the couple needed to take the next three years very seriously in terms of cleaning up their credit and paying down the debt that has been following them like a black cloud. Plus they needed the time to add to their initial $6,500 down payment. Through their monthly payments, Maria and Daniel were going to accumulate a $26,500 down payment credit. Which was about 10 percent of the future price of the house ($265,000).

Maria was determined to get her family's financial situation under control and on a better track. She decided to open a home-based business. The extra income she generated allowed her to chisel away at the debt faster. She then consolidated the rest of their debt. This made it easier to make frequent payments. Plus she started to pay bills on time, in some cases even earlier than the monthly statements arrived. By Christmas time, for the first time in years she saw her credit score start to rise. That was the motivation she needed to keep going.

After only two years in the rent to own program, Maria accumulated just over $20,000 towards the down payment. She decided to meet with a mortgage broker in her area to go over the numbers. This mortgage broker was not affiliated with our rent to own program, and was unfamiliar with rent to own, for the most part. Maria admitted she was a little nervous that the mortgage broker would say her monthly down payment credits would not add up or not count.

After talking to the mortgage agent, Maria was in shock. She told us later that she almost fainted.

What she found out was that her and Daniel could actually qualify for a mortgage now. Not a year from now, as she originally planned. With about eight percent down, hardly any debt, good household income and credit scores of 644 and 651, all of the pieces were in place. All of their hard work had paid off. The finish line was now in sight. What a relief Maria felt.

Unfortunately, the agreements Maria and Daniel signed with the investor were for three years. Besides, the investor was locked into a three-year mortgage and the future purchase price was also based on three years.

After some convincing on our part, the investor was willing to reduce the purchase price to let the couple buy the house a year earlier than originally agreed. The investor's bank was going to charge him a penalty for discharging the mortgage early, and if Maria was willing to cover the expense, he was game. Maria agreed, and put aside extra money over the next two months to cover the bank's penalty. With penalty money in hand, Maria gathered all of their mortgage application documents together and successfully secured a mortgage for the house her and Daniel rented to own.

Maria and her father, about one year before he passed away. He was the inspiration for Maria to start building up a nest egg for her three kids. After only two years into her three-year rent to own arrangement, Maria and her husband were able to qualify for a mortgage early and are now on title of the home they rented to own.

Looking back, Maria told us that she remembers feeling embarrassed when her dying father pointed out that she wasting her money on rent. That same feeling helped to change the course of her life. In the rent to own program, Maria accomplished more in two years than she had in the past eight years. She increased her income, changed payment habits, downloaded her credit report every six months to make sure the bureau was capturing accurate information and also to see if her credit score was going up. The nudge from her dad helped Maria take action. The rent to own program made Maria more accountable. She recognized that she had more on the line than before, which helped her stay focused and work hard. In the end Maria reached the finish line and in her heart she knew her dad was proudly applauding her accomplishment.

How motivated are you to have your very own home? Can you see yourself in it? What does the image look like to you? Hold that thought! Perfect the image in your mind daily. The more seriously you want to be a homeowner, the more vivid your mental picture will get, the sooner your dream will come true.

"Everything is created twice. First with imagination in your mind. Second, when it manifests in your material world." – Bob Proctor

Glossary of Terms

If you are considering homeownership for the first time, you may be overwhelmed with some of the language you hear realtors or mortgage professionals use. For your reference, we included a brief definition of some of the key terms you should be familiar with. This list is not intended to be exhaustive, just a sampling of common words.

APPRECIATION

Appreciation is the increase in value of a certain asset over time. Many types of assets appreciate, including stocks, commodities and real estate. When you purchase a home, you not only provide yourself with a place to live, but gain an asset that has the potential to increase in value over time. Home appreciation can be expressed several ways, such as the total dollar value increase over a certain period or as an average value increase per year over a certain period.

ASSET

In financial accounting, assets are economic resources. Anything tangible or intangible that is capable of being owned or controlled to produce value and that is held to have positive economic value is considered an asset. Simply stated, assets represent value of ownership that can be converted into cash (although cash itself is also considered an asset).[11]

CLOSING COSTS

Real property in most jurisdictions is conveyed from the seller to the buyer through a real estate contract. The point in time at which the contract is actually executed and the title to the property is conveyed to the buyer is known as the "closing". It is common for a variety of costs associated with the transaction (above and beyond the price of the property itself) to be incurred by either the buyer or the seller. These costs are typically paid at the closing, and are known as closing costs.[12]

---

[11] Source: Wikipedia
[12] Source: Wikipedia

COLLATERAL

In lending agreements, collateral is a borrower's pledge of specific property to a lender, to secure repayment of a loan. The collateral serves as protection for a lender against a borrower's default - that is, any borrower failing to pay the principal and interest under the terms of a loan obligation. If a borrower does default on a loan (due to insolvency or other event), that borrower forfeits (gives up) the property pledged as collateral - and the lender then becomes the owner of the collateral. In a typical mortgage loan transaction, for instance, the real estate being acquired with the help of the loan serves as collateral. Should the buyer fail to pay the loan under the mortgage loan agreement, the ownership of the real estate is transferred to the bank. The bank uses a legal process called foreclosure to obtain real estate from a borrower who defaults on a mortgage loan obligation.[13]

HOME EQUITY

Your home equity is the value of your home less all debts you might have on the home. Your debts would include mortgage, home equity loan, and home equity line of credit. When you retire, your home equity can become an important financial asset, especially if you sell your home and buy a less expensive place to live. If your home is worth $250,000, your mortgage is $150,000, your home equity loan is $25,000 and you have no home equity line, your home equity is $75,000 ($250,000 - $150,000 - $25,000 = $75,000).[14]

LEVERAGE

A method of financing an investment by which an investor pays only a small percentage of the purchase price in cash, with the balance supplemented by borrowed fund, in order to generate a greater rate of return than would be produced by paying with 100 percent of personal cash for the investment.

OPTION PREMIUM

The homebuyer is able to rent the home for a specified period of time. But that rent is not just rent; a portion of the monthly payment is set aside as a credit for an eventual purchase of the house. The amount that is set aside as a credit is known as the option premium.

STATED INCOME

Stated income is the amount of income the borrower attests to having, and which can be supported with documents such as tax returns, notices of assessment, contracts and financial statements.

---

[13] Source: Wikipedia
[14] Source: About.com

Ready. Go.

Remember, with the purchase of this book, you also receive *Rent to Own Essential Tools for Homebuyers*, a bonus collection of action-oriented worksheets to help you get on the path of homeownership faster. These free tools are designed to provide shortcuts to making your homeownership goals a reality in record time.

You can request your bonus material by emailing: **info@renting2own.ca**.

Printed in Great Britain
by Amazon